The Road Spoke

The
Road
Spoke

TREPIDATION AND TRANQUILITY ON A BICYCLE ODYSSEY

K. R. REINKE

Publishing Services provided by Paper Raven Books LLC
Printed in the United States of America
First Printing, 2024

Paperback ISBN: 979-8-9905700-0-9
Hardback ISBN: 979-8-9905700-1-6

Maps created in Keynote by Author.

Table of Contents

Prologue

I completed this trip without any intention of writing a book, but then a close friend asked, "How did you do it?" He was referring to the fact that I had made a 3,700-mile bicycle trip—unescorted—as a 69-year-old polio survivor and an insulin-dependent diabetic, "while the rest of us are sitting on our couches." This book explains that, but my main purpose in completing it is to give you, the reader, an increased capacity for joy. I have included tools that I use.

You will also know what it is like to ride a bike solo across the United States.

When I was 12, I looked in the mirror and saw a 12-year-old boy. I am sure I had judgments about what I was looking at. Now, when I look in the mirror, I see an old man. But this old man understands that there are two entities at play—the one that sees and the one that judges. This is an essential distinction.

To the Essence

CHAPTER 1

Travelmania

It is a stunning morning in Hawthorne, Florida, and I am going to ride my bicycle over to my friend Frank's house. My bike is loaded for an epic ride—four panniers full of stuff and a handlebar bag. I have everything I need to get to Frank's house: tent, sleeping mats, sleeping bag, spare biking outfit, street clothes, food, water, and a credit card. I also have bicycle repair tools, spare inner tubes, a tire pump, two light jackets (layers), and two pairs of socks.

I can't carry all the food and water that I need to get to Frank's, but I will start out with a jar of nut butter, a jar of jelly, a large pack of tortillas, a case of meal bars, and three liters of water. I also have an empty Camelback bladder that I will fill for crossing the areas where water will be in short supply.

I need all this stuff to get to Frank's house because I live in Hawthorne, Florida, and he lives in Port Townsend, Washington. There are at least 3,500 miles of road between us. My intention is to cover the entire distance pedaling "Truckee," my touring bicycle.

Starting out, my panniers and gear will total 50 pounds. Truckee weighs 45 pounds, and I weigh around 200 pounds. One needs a lot of stuff to cover that kind of distance on a bicycle including gumption. We will see if I have enough of it later. There is a clue that I might have it.

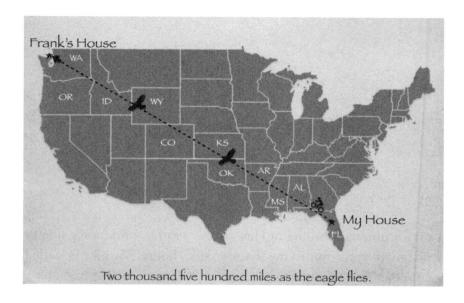

Two thousand five hundred miles as the eagle flies.

But let's say you are sitting at your kitchen table and for some crazy reason you decide you want to try to ride your bicycle from Florida to the state of Washington.

When on Earth would you depart? It would take months to make the trip—perhaps three. If you leave too early, there could be freezing cold during the beginning of the trip. There could even be snow. And if you traverse the northwestern states too early in the year, that threat is redoubled. If you leave too late, riding through the plains and prairie states could be like bicycling through a furnace.

I started my cross-country cycling (XC cycling) a little late in life. I have always enjoyed bicycling. I loved quietly covering different terrain under my own power. I loved hiking also—back when I could walk. The quiet was why I also gravitated toward canoeing and kayaking. Motorized transportation was only a way to get to quiet forays.

2

But cross-country cycling requires lots of time, and who has that prior to retirement? Well… it turns out that I did, but I spent it doing other things. I have had a yen for traveling, which carried me to Alaska earlier in my life. For many years I went to Kodiak, Alaska most summers to work in the salmon-processing industry. Early in the spring, I would show up at what became one of my "homes." It was a remote salmon cannery in Uganik Bay on Kodiak Island. There, I would be put up in a bunkhouse and fed in the mess hall for the summer. I would work a minimum of 68 hours per week and as many as 106.

There was nothing around the cannery except bushes and bears. There wasn't anywhere to spend your money except on the meager provisions at the company store. The cannery was built at the base of a steep mountain, and there were no roads. The only trails were made by animals. Kodiak Brown Bears make nice trails, but it is off-putting to most people to use them.

The company flew me up from Seattle in the spring and flew me back to Seattle in the fall. I would work there for three or four months, and in September, I would leave with all the money I had made through the summer. Rich, say, by college student standards. After months of being anchored up in that small, self-contained facility, I was free to begin moving again. Many times, I would make my way back to my other "home" in Sarasota, Florida—often by hitchhiking. Consequently, I have hitchhiked over 16,000 miles in the United States.

During my years working in Alaska, my penchant for travel kicked into overdrive. I discovered backpack traveling in foreign countries. It did not end for me until I had passed through 30 different countries. I found that my money would last much longer if I took my time in third-world or what they now call "developing" countries.

I became very familiar with hardship traveling and, in fact, found it preferable. Very little of my hard-earned money was spent while traveling. The asperity of traveling by poorer methods and in poorer countries allowed me to see many places unsullied by popular travel.

I met many people similarly unsullied. In any nation, when traveling in popular tourist areas, you meet a different kind of local than you do in the open countryside. I guess that is one reason I took to XC cycling after my retirement.

CHAPTER 2

Polio and Other
Menacing Doubts

I was born in 1951 during a polio epidemic. Poliomyelitis is a viral disease that can affect nerve cells. Most people who were exposed suffered flu-like symptoms or none at all. Within a year, I managed to fall into the 1 or 2 percent that suffered some paralysis. I suppose you could call it a mild case. I only suffered leg-muscle atrophy. Many people had it much worse, and many died.

Because of the polio, I have walked with a limp for my entire life. Doctors disagreed on the extent of my remaining disability. Mild muscular atrophy in left leg was one diagnosis. Both legs said another. At any rate, both of my calves are skinny, one more than the other.

Humans seem capable of getting used to anything given enough time. I played all sports in gym classes, but none all that well. I was picked last for most. That was a given. In baseball I could hit a ball farther than anyone, but it took hitting it over the fielder's head to give me enough time to get to first base. One time, I was on second base (God knows how I got there), and the batter hit what would amount to an infield home run. He rounded third base, and I was still less than halfway from third to the home plate. He caught up to me, picked me up, and carried me across the plate.

Walking through hallways during my school years with a squeaking leg brace was pretty terrible. However, this early suffering could be the reason I persevere through adversity as you will see from this story. I'll leave that one up to the psychologists among you. I'm not boasting—I'm as amazed as anyone might be—and still trying to figure it all out. With one leg slightly shorter and having limped my entire life, I am left with a painful scoliosis that will no longer allow me to stand for any length of time or walk any distance without a cane. However, I can sit on my bicycle seat for hours and days without pain.

But what about crossing the country on a bicycle? When would you leave Florida? I already had some experience with this. When I retired to Hawthorne, Florida, I bought two used mountain bikes. I know… mountain bikes in Florida. Turns out they are great for crappy roads, trails, and they are not too terrible in sand. I needed all the help I could get. My leg strength seemed to be diminishing over time—possibly from post-polio syndrome. It turns out that if you live long enough after polio, you can suffer a latent deterioration. I had been working for the last seven years in Kodiak as the director of a nonprofit. Though I had a mountain bike in Alaska, the weather on Kodiak Island did not lend itself to an old guy riding a bicycle for much of the year. I could no longer make the hills. Nor are the winters on Kodiak Island favorable for getting any outside exercise for a person who now walks with a cane. Thus, retiring to Florida seemed pragmatic.

The flatter terrain of north Florida and the delicious lack of snow and ice was perfect for getting back into biking. Riding eight miles round trip to one of the nearby convenience stores felt like plenty of exercise at first. Over a year's time, eight miles turned into 13, then 20. Once again, persistence paid off. The first time I did 30 miles, though, I thought to myself that it was too much. I was exhausted.

Nevertheless, getting up early to avoid the heat and the fabulous freedom of traveling quietly on county roads suited me. Before long, I could comfortably ride 30 miles in a morning session. My neural pathways being what they are, I started to think about the idea of crossing the country by bicycle. It came on like something I couldn't help. But I told no one. I wondered about the sanity of it. I was 67 years old at the time of that first trip and had long ago added being an insulin-dependent diabetic to my list of impediments.

Of course, there would have been a certain amount of prudence in traveling with someone. But I did not know anyone who rode a bicycle as much as I did. And I did not want to be held back any more than I would want to hold someone else back. For me, going it alone would be key even if foolish.

Taking a shorter, practice road trip might have made more sense. Perhaps a ride across the Florida Panhandle or down to Key West. In this case I was just suffering from thinking big.

At the time, my wife was still working in Alaska, and I eventually leaked it to her that I had this crazy idea. Since she is sane and kind, her comment was that it seemed too far. My friend Brad in Gainesville, Florida thought it was a little bit crazy, but he was supportive. He said that if I got down the road a bit and felt like it was a mistake, he would come and get me.

With a rescue already lined up, I forged ahead. I tried to outfit my mountain bike for long-distance travel but realized quickly that it wasn't going to work. The mountain bike was wobbly with weight on it, and, as I discovered later, the suspension causes a terrific loss of efficiency. The comfort of the mountain bike precludes long-distance travel for us old, gimpy guys. I guess it was lucky for me that I didn't realize at first that doing 30-mile trips on a mountain bike was good conditioning for a road trip.

If I was going to commit to this strenuous trip, I needed to put the odds in my favor. Procuring a touring bike was in order. Mountain bikes are usually aluminum-framed, and they usually have suspension on one or both wheels to give comfort over rough terrain. Touring bikes are usually steel-framed without suspension and are geared low for carrying heavy loads over long distances. I looked for a used touring bike for quite a while but couldn't find one that fit. If you are just dinking around on a bike, the fit is less important. You can get by on a frame size that is not perfect. If you are going to travel weeks on end, a bike that fits your body frame is paramount.

My research brought me to Bikes and More in Gainesville, and I found myself ordering a Surly Long-Haul Trucker that was fitted for me. It was well out of budget and the only new bike I'd ordered in 40 years, but I have never regretted that decision.

Once I picked up my brand-new bicycle, I started riding it exclusively. People sometimes name their bikes. I never had, but calling this one Truckee seemed apropos since the bike was a Long-Haul <u>Trucker</u>. I was on my way to being on my way. Riding it without a load felt like it was geared too low, but it was so much faster than my mountain bike. Right away, I had my first lesson in bicycle efficiency. The same distance that took an hour and 10 minutes on my mountain bike took about 50 minutes on Truckee. Without suspension, though, the rough trails and bad roads were no longer appropriate. Now the mission was training for riding across the country.

I wasn't sure of a route, so I joined the Adventure Cycling Association. They have over 40,000 miles of route maps made especially for bicycling. There are three major routes for crossing the country. I chose the "Southern Tier," which takes seven maps from St. Augustine, Florida to San Diego, California. The trail passes within 15 miles of my house. Their maps are broken down into 30-mile sections, giving the user a great idea of what to expect ahead even though it could well be nothing. They follow low-traffic routes as much as they can and guide you through cities where necessary. They show services along the way including towns with libraries, tourist stops, motels, campgrounds, and country convenience stores. Bike shops are marked along all the routes. They take a wonderful amount of guesswork out of a trip. Also, their magazine and other resources are excellent for planning the adventure.

During training, I was halfway through a 26-mile ride and started to feel my blood sugar go low. There are numbers that diabetics learn. Numbers of which most non-diabetics are completely and blessedly unaware. In the simplest terms, a non-diabetic's body keeps the blood sugar between 70 and 125 when fasting and somewhat higher after a meal. A miraculous combination of mechanisms in the body keeps blood sugar in that range. When these mechanisms break down, those numbers can go completely out of whack and cause a plethora of difficulties. Taking too much medication—in my case insulin—can send me into a low blood sugar spiral, as can too much exercise. This calls for constant monitoring and adjusting for diet and exercise. This started for me in my 40s, so I had been at it for quite a while. On this afternoon of training, some unusual circumstances led to unanticipated consequences.

"Going low" is a regular occurrence for me, and I am always prepared for it. All it takes to rectify the situation is to consume sugar in some form. I carry gel packets with me all the time. I might forget to put some in my pocket, but I always have several taped to the bicycle. When the low feeling comes over me, a packet gets me out of any immediate danger. Then I must find some real food to keep me out of danger, as going too low for too long puts one in a coma.

There was a convenience store about five miles ahead where I would be able to purchase some fruit to better situate me along my internal insulin/carbohydrate continuum. Halfway to the store, I stopped at the Ochwilla Elementary School for a break. The school was a regular rest stop for me during the summer when it was closed. There were very few people around, a water spigot outdoors, and nice benches for resting. I had a friendly, nodding acquaintance with the women I would sometimes encounter there. On this occasion I didn't have to worry if I started going low again as I had plenty of gel packets.

I unrolled my resting pad on the ground. This was a pretty long ride for me at the time, and it felt good to lie on the pad and put my feet up on a bench. I was in the shade and enjoying the perfect morning temperature. I called my brother on my cell phone, and we yukked it up for a while. When I hung up, I laid the phone on my chest to take a blissful little nap... that led into a diabetic coma.

When I am awake, I can always feel the onset of low blood sugar. It announces itself in the form of shakiness, lightheadedness, and sometimes mild confusion. As a diabetic, the first line of defense is always sugar. I have trained myself that no matter what unusual feeling I might have, I need to get some sugar in there. It cannot get better on its own, and a little confusion leads to a lot of confusion, making it more difficult to remember the sugar. If it comes on while I am in my sleep, someone else must step in.

When I started to come around, there was a policeman standing over me and three or four ladies from the school standing behind him. I came to slowly and steadily. I heard myself asking him where I was. He said I was at the Ochwilla School, but I couldn't make sense of it. It sounded like an Alaskan name to me, but I was pretty sure I wasn't in Alaska. I was aware that I was coming out of a diabetic coma, but not much else was plausible yet. I had a Gu packet in my hand, and I was bewildered by the fact that the police carried the same brand and flavor that I carried. Each of those wonderful ladies was holding some form of sugary snack in their hand to help me come around.

I do not know how long I had lain outside the school, but at some point, one of the women checked on me, couldn't wake me up, and called the police. When the policeman arrived, he picked up my cell phone and saw that I had a missed call, and he hit redial. My wife had called twice, but I did not hear the phone ring. The policeman ended up talking to the perfect person to deal with my situation. She told him what was up and that he needed to get sugar in me. I guess the police do not carry Gu Packets. She had told him about the ones taped to my bike.

The policeman had called for an ambulance. Though there was an ambulance station about two blocks away, they were out on a call. My ambulance was coming from halfway across the county. By the time the paramedics showed up, my cognition had returned enough for me to refuse going to the hospital. I had some experience with this, and I knew that once I was back in the world, there wasn't much more they could do for me at a hospital. Any damage was done. I was more afraid of the damage the hospital would do to my wallet.

After that incident, I spent a few days thinking that riding a bicycle across the country in my condition would be stupid. If I suffered a coma in some out-of-the-way place—like the woods—I could very well not recover.

But that thinking only lasted a couple of days. I cooked up a diabetic plan instead. There would be no napping during the day unless I had eaten a substantial meal, and no taking insulin at night. Also, getting that much exercise every day called for a lot less insulin and a lot more carbohydrates. Careful adjustments were in order.

I still had to decide on a departure date. I had the excellent biking maps from the cycling club, so I knew which towns I would travel through. I looked at high and low temperatures and rainfall data across the route and decided that mid-February seemed like a good departure time. However, I dragged my feet on leaving. I was probably hoping that some catastrophe would occur that would stop me from taking this insane trip.

I ended up leaving my house in early March. I marched forth on March 4. During my first nights on the road, the temperature was 31 degrees, and I found myself thinking I had left too early. Later on, I would find out that I hadn't.

My trajectory on that first trip was straightforward. I would head west along the Southern Tier aiming for Phoenix, Arizona and then divert toward my brother's house in the San Francisco Bay area. It was a laudable if not laughable goal. A 3,000-mile bicycle trip for the diabetic crippled kid, 67 years old at the time. That was "Route 67."

CHAPTER 3

Departure, Route 69

Two years after Route 67, I was back at my kitchen table trying to decide on a departure date for an even more laudable and more laughable goal. More laudable in that the goal was about 700 miles farther than the first goal and I was now 69 years old. More laughable for both of those reasons as well. This book is about Route 69, but it will have references to that first adventure. For this new bicycle odyssey, I chose April 1, yes… April Fools' Day (2021) as a starting date.

I called my first XC adventure Route 67. I called this one Route 69. On Route 67 I had no experience, but I had great maps. I did not have to work hard on finding directions. On Route 69 I had a ton of experience but had to rely on regular paper maps and Google Maps Bicycle (GMB). I had no preplanned bike route. My path was connect-the-dots. I had friends that would put me up in Jackson, Mississippi; Tulsa, Oklahoma; Centennial, Colorado; and I wanted to make a stop at the Adventure Cycling Association in Missoula, Montana. After that, the intended final stop was Frank's house in Port Townsend, Washington. I just had to figure out all the in-between bits as I went.

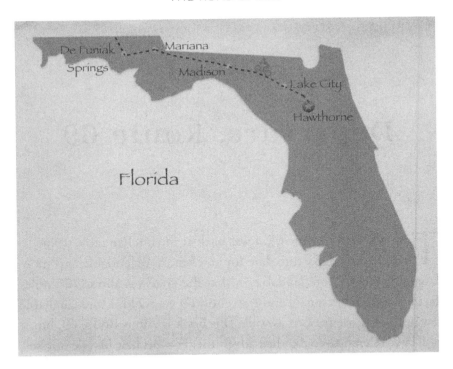

Once again, I found myself—at first light on a beautiful morning—steering my touring bike with 50 pounds of gear out of my carport. I was pedaling away from my perfectly adequate heated and air-conditioned domicile. Leaving my cozy bed and my yard where I loved to putter, away from all the conveniences anyone would really need. The long goal was Frank's house in Washington, but I had a few "escape hatches." The first was Brad in Gainesville, who had once again pledged to come and rescue me if I got into trouble in Florida or Alabama. The second was my friends' place in Jackson, Mississippi 600 miles away. That was my first planned big stop. I had decided that when I got there, if I did not feel like continuing, I could rent a car that would fit my bike and all my junk and just drive back to Florida. This was my fallback plan if I had to give up anywhere near a rental car in Alabama or Mississippi.

My next planned stop after that was 1,250 miles farther at my brother-in-law's house in Centennial, Colorado. If I made it that far and had to quit, I would most likely ship my bicycle back and fly home.

What would give me the idea that I could even possibly make that kind of mileage? Well, because I had made that kind of mileage on my first trip. But not without learning an important lesson early on.

The journey of a thousand miles begins with a single step.

— *Tao Te Ching*

On my first cross-country trip—Route 67—I managed to get myself on the road, but I was not armed with the proper wisdom. I was thinking that since I could ride 30 miles in a morning on an empty bike, I would be able to manage another 30 over the entire rest of the day. Given some breaks and caveats, at that rate the trip would take around two-and-a-half months. Never mind that I had yet to ride 30 miles at one time on my fully loaded bike. In fact, I hadn't trained at full weight at all.

On the first day of my first cross-country trip—Route 67—I rode 40 miles to Brad's house in Gainesville where I spent a very comfortable first night. My second and third days out involved 31-degree nights and headwinds of at least eight miles per hour all day. I was comfortable at night in my down sleeping bag with my two mats, but the days were tedious and not very fun. I wasn't making near the time I had hoped. Was my trip going to take a whole month longer than I expected? Because of this kind of thinking, I pushed harder, and before long, my knee was hurting. I was further dispirited and started to crash mentally. The challenge of that first trip was catching up to me.

That night in my tent, I had to make the call. Rather than call Brad for the promised bail out, I called Dara, a friend in South Florida who is a triathlete trainer by profession. I whined to her for a while about my knee, and her sage advice still sounds in my head. "Stop pushing. Use your gears."

The next day, I rode 40 miles to Marianna, Florida and took a cheap motel room. I slept well that night and the next day woke up with a new, important, game-changing perspective. I had heard Dara and carried her advice to a powerful conclusion. The goal had gotten in the way. I did not have to make 60 miles a day. That was just a ridiculous expectation that I had foisted upon myself. In fact, I did not have to make it to California or even Arizona or Louisiana. I only had to make it to the top of the next hill in front of me. And then only one step (pedal) at a time. The goal had taken over, and I almost talked myself into quitting in the first six days. The impediment was not physical—it was mental! I had plenty of challenges ahead, but this one ended here. I had to remind myself several times, but it came easily once I internalized this truth. I found in Lao Tzu's wisdom that every step is a first step. The smaller the time interval you track in your mind, the easier the journey becomes.

That first trip, Route 67, taught me well. I learned that we throw a tremendous amount of hardship and suffering on ourselves just with our minds. We are almost never taught that we don't have to. In fact, we are taught the opposite. That will become clearer further along this journey.

The trip this book covers—Route 69, heading for Port Townsend—was unburdened, except for short intervals, by the thoughts of mileage and timing. My prospective hosts in Jackson were kind enough to accept an estimated time of arrival at 10 to 17 days. When you are traveling by bicycle, there are just too many things that can mutilate a schedule. Wind and rain are chief among them. Hills, heat, and cold can disfigure plans as well.

Although the departure date of this trip was influenced by its celebrity, my hope was to get across the plains and prairies before it got too hot. I further hoped to avoid getting into the northwestern states before it had quit snowing. At some of the higher elevations, that can be questionable most of the year.

My route to Port Townsend was decidedly undecided. The Adventure Cycling Association has no route maps that cross the country from the Southeast to the Northwest. I would only overlap with a few small pieces of their routes. I had to wing it. I had in mind that I would do whatever it took to go northwest to Jackson, Mississippi, then northwest to Centennial, Colorado and then northwest to Missoula, Montana. I chose Missoula, Montana as a destination because the home office of the American Cycling Association is located there. It is a bicycling Mecca. If I made it that far, I would then choose which road I would take over the continental divide. I would use paper maps and Google Maps Bicycle (GMB) in combination. There would be plenty of surprises.

I was faced with a lot of headwinds on the first day of Route 69. Also, early on, I got lost on some back roads. I wasn't sure if it was GMB or if I had misread the thing. It would be the first of many routing debacles.

I had to push my heavy load for about a mile through sand where the road had deteriorated. Then the road ended at someone's house. Rather than push back the mile through the sand trap, I found a locked gate into what looked like public land, and I dragged my bike under it. I have talked to many XC bikers who also thought that backtracking was the last option.

I eventually ran into a logger who knew the area, and he helped get me on the Palatka/Lake Butler Trail. It is a rails-to-trails route that is beautifully paved between Palatka and Keystone Heights, Florida. By this time, though, it had deteriorated into a forest track and then further into a path that looked like they had just barely pulled up the railroad tracks. It would have been a great ride on my unloaded mountain bike, but on Truckee it was dreadful. I was nearly shaken and vibrated to death by the time I got to Lake Butler.

Perhaps this would be a good time to discuss bicycle seats. When talking to non-cyclists about long-distance riding, most people bring up how uncomfortable that skinny seat must be. It turns out that if you get the right seat, it is not uncomfortable at all. However, it is certainly difficult to find the right seat. In one article on the subject, the writer suggested buying 30 "saddles" and returning 29 of them. It is almost that difficult to get the perfect seat. I lucked out on my first XC saddle, but it was worn out when that trip ended. That saddle was out of production, and I had to settle for getting as close as I could on the new one. The replacement wasn't quite as great, but it was good. Contrary to popular, non-cyclist belief, a big, fat, cushy saddle will likely end your trip early due to chafing. The skinny saddle is a must. Once you get used to the right saddle, you hardly notice it.

Another integral part of making the long distance is your bike shorts. You must experiment with them also. I bought "lightly padded" biking shorts that were far too padded for me. It felt like sitting on a diaper. I went to an online forum for an answer, and "triathlete shorts" were suggested. I bought a pair and found them far less padded and the perfect solution for me. A well-constructed pair of shorts can mean the difference between finishing a trip happily and dropping out or finishing in misery. Over the course of traveling thousands of miles and in myriad weather conditions, you are bound to encounter some chafing. I always have a tube of petroleum jelly for such occasions. Of course, your shorts must withstand that too.

Oh, and how many pairs? Two. There is a delicate balance between traveling light and traveling comfortably. More on that later.

CHAPTER 4

Stealth Camping

So, on my first day of Route 69, I stopped riding at 58 miles. I was just past the town of Lake Butler, Florida. Cross-country cyclists that suffer from pecuniary challenges engage in something called "stealth" camping. The idea is to pay as little money as possible day to day. These days, private campgrounds can cost around $15 to $30 per night just to set up a tent. Add that up over two-and-a-half or three months and your trip costs escalate. I prefer to stealth camp and spend money on an occasional motel. Besides, on a trip like this, there are many times that you are not in range of a campground or a motel or anything. Another option is to go on a "supported" trip where your gear is carried for you in a vehicle, and you have only to ride the bike. I love the thought of this, but for me it is out of the question.

I did a lot of stealth camping back in my hitchhiking days. That translated to either me being good at it, or that most of the wonderful people in this country just don't care. If you see a bicycle and a tent behind a church or volunteer fire department, they are most likely harmless. In turn, I hope fellow stealth campers will not leave a mess.

The place I found for my first night seemed to be an abandoned Forest Service area. The spot was perfect. There was a fire watchtower and no evidence that it had been used in recent history. The lock on the tower gate was rusted shut. I set up my one-person tent, and a little later, a wild turkey ran through my camp. Was it a sign? They are the bird equivalent of the quintessential stealth camper.

I never cook. Cooking fires draw too much attention. During my research, I asked an experienced traveler what to use for cooking gear. He said to me somewhat condescendingly, "Eat cold food!" So, on this trip I will not be talking about that kind of camping. The kind where you get up and make coffee in the morning and have breakfast at the comfort of a picnic table. If I can get to a restaurant that is still serving breakfast, you might hear about veggie omelets. But you are more likely to hear about gas station coffee and gas station burritos. Believe me, no matter what or how much you eat on a trip like this, you are going to lose weight. And when you are traversing hot country, you do not want to waste the cool hours of the morning making coffee or breakfast. You need to be riding.

I often have bananas. I usually have tortillas with some kind of nut butter or jelly. Tortillas travel well. You can roll them up for weeks and still make them work. I always pack meal bars as well because there is plenty of time traveling through areas where there is nothing. On my first trip, I passed a sign in Texas that read, "Next Services 88 miles." That could be intimidating to someone in a car, much less someone on a bicycle.

For now, though, I would be traveling for weeks through the southeastern states, and services should be regular. When I am at home, I am a bit of a coffee snob, but on the road, I would drink any coffee out of any gas station and use any creamer. A coffee addiction is to be respected.

There was no rain in the forecast this night, so I did not put my rainfly on the tent. The tent itself was mostly screen on the upper half, and it was a joy to see the stars at night, and to watch the mosquitoes bounce along the outside trying to find their way in. It was April 1, and it was expected to be cool. The rainfly might help some, but my down sleeping bag, which was 20 years old, still served me well. I recommend a down bag for weight, but, of course, if it gets wet, it is useless. I have waterproof panniers, so it certainly cannot get wet during riding.

58 miles.

I spent 12 hours in the tent on my first night. Partly because the nights in April are long. But also, because I have learned to not be in a hurry and that a good rest is essential—especially at the start of a trip. Some stealth camps do not lend themselves to long mornings lying around, but this one was perfect for it. Besides, it was only 39 degrees when I woke up.

I traveled through Lake City in the early afternoon. My mission there was to find a place to eat where I could also charge my phone.

I had found during Route 67 that charging a phone could be a real issue. I spent a lot of time on that trip searching for electrical outlets where I could loiter. For this trip I was carrying a solar-charging battery device on my handlebar. I needed more charging power now because I was running Google Maps and an app called Strava. Strava follows my phone by satellite and allows my friends to keep track of me. Both of those apps use a lot of power, so I still needed plug-in charging as often as possible. I was only then finding out that the solar-charged battery device wasn't working at all. I eventually replaced the device with a larger, heavier one, but it was only barely adequate even on blindingly sunny days.

I found a pizza joint and went in. I don't usually allow myself pizza in my real life. I love it, but it is a lot of carbohydrates and is not high on the good-food list for diabetics. During XC biking, though, the carbs are burned quickly and aren't such a problem. I once met a XC cyclist gal who laughed and said, "Beer and ice cream for breakfast if you want."

I was a stranger to this style of pizza restaurant. A service person goes along an assembly line with you, and you choose what you want on it—kind of like a Subway. I didn't mind the time it took since I had found an electric outlet, and my phone was plugged in. But I was quite disappointed when leaving to discover that the electric outlet wasn't working and that my phone did not charge at all. A reminder to pay closer attention.

There was a Starbucks next door, and they always have plug-ins, but this was during COVID, and they were not allowing customers to sit inside. I was desperate, so I ordered a coffee and plugged my phone in inside and then sat at a table outside. You might notice these days that normally when someone sits by themselves in public, they are usually staring at their phone. It is just the way the world is now. The ability to sit content without having to be entertained is slipping further from us at a great cost.

It is difficult to believe that when I was young, the phones were attached to a wall and rarely used for long-distance calls. And if you wanted to look up information, you would have to go to an encyclopedia set or the library. When my family had acquired our first television, it was black and white, and since we lived near Chicago, we could get a whopping four channels—but only if you could get the rabbit ear antennas adjusted just right. If you were interested in televised news, you could see it for an hour in the six to nine p.m. time range. Yes, I grew up in ancient history. I wonder what crossing the country on a bicycle was like back then. Paper maps only. No GPS.

I have several apps on my phone that I find very useful. Aside from the two already mentioned, I regularly use a wind app (Windy.com), a weather radar app, and a second map app. I have yet to use the fancier (more expensive) Garmin or other bicycle navigation devices. This is where I draw the line. I have always loved paper maps and used them exclusively on my hitchhiking odysseys and world traveling. They are becoming a thing of the past like black-and-white televisions… and me.

After a nice long lunch and rest, including getting coffeed up and charging the phone, I vacated Lake City heading west on Highway 90. I had traveled a long way on Highway 100 getting up to Lake City. It was almost perfectly flat and perfectly straight. Highway 90 has a gentle, easy contour but is somewhat trafficky. No, there is no such word as trafficky, but a lot of distance cyclists use it often.

There are clear tradeoffs on route choices. If you want to make headway and use straighter roads with gentle grades, you are going to suffer more cars, trucks, camper vehicles, semis, and all manner of road users. On roads between points that are popular for travel, there is usually more engineering. They take the hilltops off and fill in the in-between. It makes the gradients easier for cyclists, but there is usually more traffic. The cyclist eschewing these shortcuts must work harder on hilly roads but are rewarded with a more peaceful experience.

I much prefer the quieter back roads, but I have limitations. Polio left me unable to stand up on the pedals of a bike. I cannot power-grind up a hill. I can only go up as far as I can sitting in the saddle. Then I must get off and push the bicycle the rest of the way. It can be tedious with a loaded bike, but I do it a lot.

In Wellborn, Florida I intersected with my ACA Southern Tier route map. I had used it on Route 67, and I brought it along this time to help me traverse back roads as much as possible getting to DeFuniak Springs. I consider Highway 90 "not terrible" since Interstate 10 relieved it of much congestion. But I was grateful to get away from it for a while on County Road 137.

The other difference between the busy thoroughfares and the quiet back roads is the width of the road shoulder. Highway 90 had a decent shoulder where you could ride relatively safely on pavement that was out of the traffic lane. It is needed where there is steady traffic. This county road had no shoulder but very few cars. Occasionally on these back roads, I sometimes get "twixted." That is when the rare overtaking vehicle meets the rare oncoming vehicle right where I happen to be on a narrow or nonexistent road shoulder. Every cyclist talks about times where there was no traffic for miles, and then suddenly, there is a car or truck from each direction at the same time. It is a cyclist's variation of Murphy's Law.

Back at my home in Putnam County, I rode thousands of miles on roads with a 14-inch-wide shoulder. If everyone is paying attention—motorists and cyclist—it is safe to ride. Of course, a small inattention can lead to wretched consequences for the cyclist. It is the law in Florida that a driver must allow a minimum of three feet when passing a cyclist. Sometimes I think I might be the only person in Florida, save a few cyclists, who knows about that law. I suppose that is why my neighbors often told me they thought I was crazy. Some said brave. Some, stupid.

CHAPTER 5

Dog Gone

I stopped for the night along County Road 132. People I meet along the way often ask me where I will spend the night. I tell them that they would have to ask me around 6 p.m. because that is when I start looking for an adequate, surreptitious campsite. If I see an area that looks good, I'll stop. Around 7 p.m., I will be looking more desperately and settle for a less-than-perfect, less-clandestine site.

Since I have this mobility issue from polio, it is very difficult for me to push the bike across a ditch or through any hazards like fences or brush. Ideally, I will find a place where a dirt road crosses the ditch where there are no mailboxes and without "no trespassing" signs. I can pedal in and then walk my bike into the woods to a nice flat spot that is not easily seen from the main road. A good stealth camp is a treat.

When I find such a road, I consider how well used it looks and how close to the weekend it is. If it looks well used and it is close to a weekend, then I walk my bike deeper into the woods to hide better. I am all for people having their fun. I just don't want to become part of it.

If such a spot does not present itself, then I will watch for a church or volunteer fire department with no houses behind them. The rural fire departments are rarely occupied. I'm not usually seen and always hope that if I am, forgiveness will reign. Ironically, at one church in North Florida, I was spotted and kicked out. I had to pack up my camp and head down the road in the retreating light to find another place.

In that case it was too late to find something good, and I ended up dragging my bike across a ditch and into the woods about 100 yards from a house with barky dogs. I find that once a dog spots or hears you, it will not let it go easily. After all, that is the dog's job, and they are usually good at it.

Tonight, I had found a spot closer to ideal. I was in short biking range of crossing the Suwannee River. I stopped a little early because once I crossed the Suwannee, I would be back on Highway 90, and it would be more difficult to find a good stealth camp.

43 miles.

Crazy. Brave. Stupid. To someone timid or very risk-averse, yes, riding a bicycle across the country could seem crazy. I do not think I am crazy, though I don't see any possible profit from putting the question before my wife.

Brave is not a good word either. Bravery applies to people who feel fear and move forward anyway. I lack fear about these trips. I feel like no one wants to run me over—if not from compassion, then at least for knowing how inconvenient it would be for them. I must admit that a time or two this theory came into question. I assume that the many distracted drivers will notice me up ahead and put their cell phones down until they pass me. It's a nice thought. I think intrepid is a better word for XC cyclists. They assume there are risks known and unknown but are willing to face them.

Stupid is a judgement more based on the outcome. It is a stupid risk until you have made it across the country. I guess this trip is even more stupid since I am a 69-year-old gimp. I will use gimp or gimpy throughout this book. My wife tells me it is a somewhat dated, derogatory term used to describe someone who walks with a limp. I'm reminded of an aphorism we used as children. "Sticks and stones

26

may break my bones, but words can never hurt me." So true, words cannot hurt you… unless you let them…

Enough semantics. Let's see what happens.

The wind was cooperating better on Day 3. Instead of slight, squirrelly headwinds, I got to ride with a light tailwind. Tailwinds are delicious! They are always a joy.

I just met a pair of XC cyclists that had come all the way from Waco, Texas. It was a married couple, and they still seemed to like each other. That is no small feat after facing the kind of adversity met on a long-distance bike trip.

I made a judgement error and rode through Madison, Florida without stopping for repast. The next town, Greenville, had little to choose from, and I ended up dining at a barbecue truck. I don't know if the truck needed an oil change, but the fryer sure did. I have a cast-iron gullet, but the fries had to go in the trash. Thankfully, the barbecue sandwiches were good as I had ordered two.

I was lucky again picking a stealth camp. This time, though, as I went back on the dirt road, I came to a spot where I could see an old-looking camper trailer through the brush. I was too tired to go back out on the main road, so I just backtracked a little and found a decent spot to set up my tent. It was not a well-traveled dirt road, and the trailer might have been abandoned, or a meth lab… or an abandoned meth lab.

62 miles.

On Day 4, I was dragging around in the morning. I wanted coffee, but it did not look like any was going to present itself for quite a few miles. It did not help that my inflatable mat had sprung a leak. Sleeping on the ground ain't what it used to be, so I carry two mats. One is a cheap ridge mat that I keep rolled up on the bike rack for day use. The other is an expensive self-inflating mat that I use along with the ridge mat at night. I need them both. The latter died on me. I found a leak at the valve stem, so it was nothing I could repair. It had a lifetime guarantee, but that didn't help me now. I doubted that I would find a suitable replacement before getting to Jackson, Mississippi.

I broke camp and went out on the paved road. Within a mile, I passed a yard with three loose dogs. They barked like heck, which is OK. But one of them—an intrepid one—decided to give chase.

There is something about loose dogs and bicycles. Some dogs will chase anything, but for a lot of dogs, a bicycle is irresistible. And the southeastern United States is rife with loose dogs. I have often said that in the South, loose dogs will chase a cyclist from the Atlantic Ocean to the Mississippi River.

I love dogs. I have always been the guy who will get down on the ground to play with a dog. But being chased on a bicycle is very dangerous, even for the dog if there is traffic. I've seen a lot of chats on the subject and a lot of advice. Airhorns and mace seem to be the most popular. Stopping with your bike between yourself and the dog usually works if you have enough time to get off the bike safely. One time, I had two pit bulls on me so fast that I only had time to fall over. Thankfully, they seemed to lose interest once I was on the ground straddling the bike.

For me trying to outrun a dog while on a loaded bike is the impossible dream. I have settled on carrying a spray bottle full of capsicum oil mixed with hot sauce. It is effective. But you need a spray bottle that sprays a stream a very long distance. You cannot let them get too close. I have heard of a dog grabbing a rear pannier, and even that can be devastating. Good, reliable sprayers are extremely hard to find. I use a Zep professional sprayer with excellent results. It sprays a stream about 30 feet. The problem is that it is tall and takes up a whole water bottle cage. That is quite a sacrifice for a long-distance road trip, but there you have another trade-off. Getting taken down like a wounded deer would be a greater oblation.

I have a lot of experience with this since North Florida behaves like any other southeastern state as far as dogs are concerned. You would think there were no leash laws at all in Putnam County. There might not be. I have named one of my regular routes "Five Dogs" because in a two-mile stretch, that is how many dogs that chased me in one pass. I have taken it upon myself to make my routes safer for me and any other poor souls on bikes. During my routine rides, I always have my handy bottle of special dog-repellant spray. Since I do these rides without loads, I have better maneuverability and can get to speed easier. Any dogs that give chase get sprayed, and the closer they get, the more in their face they get it.

They don't like it. It usually stops them with one contact, and once they stop chasing me, I always turn the bike around and chase them. Dogs understand pursuit, and they always run like hell. I can never catch them, but they get the point.

One fenced-in yard along the Five-Dogs route had five large dogs, three of which would squeeze under the gate to come after me. It only took a few reverse-chases before they gave up altogether. In fact, one day I was riding down the road and saw all five of them out of the yard about a half block away. I rang my bell to get their attention, and when they saw me, they ran back to the gate and squeezed under before I could get there.

Today's dog was not super interested, probably because his buddies didn't join him. I got safely past it but then discovered that I did not have my cane with me. I carry a collapsible cane on my trips to help me set up and break camp. Also, if I got into trouble and had to abandon the bike, I would be in real trouble without a cane.

I had left it at the last campsite. I went past the dogs again and found my cane and then had to pass them a third time! Each time they barked as though they were announcing Armageddon. There were people at the house, and I'm sure they thought I was crazy or an idiot (probably both) for riding back and forth past their dogs out in the countryside. Ah, life!

If anyone tells me Florida is flat, I will suggest they ride a loaded bike through Tallahassee. I had ridden through it once before, but today, it felt relentless. In 1898 there was a descriptive travel brochure about Leon County called, "Florida Hill Country."

My solar cell phone battery was not working well enough to continue carrying it. My apps were discharging my phone quickly. In Tallahassee I was able to buy a rechargeable battery that would hold about three charges. I hoped this would be enough.

I tried to get my inflatable sleeping mat replaced at a giant outdoor store, but I got there as they were closing early for Easter. For an instant I was disappointed to be traveling through a city on a Sunday. Normally, Sunday is a great day for bike riding as there is far less traffic and especially truck traffic. Navigating the hills of Tallahassee without competing for road space with trucks was a blessing. However, this cinched that I was likely to have to spend my nights on one mat until I got to Jackson, Mississippi. I pushed the rest of the way through Tallahassee so that I could be in a more rural setting come Monday morning. I called ahead to get a cheap motel room near Midway, Florida. It was imperative to spend the night near an electrical outlet to get my phone and new battery fully charged.

I like using the smaller mom-and-pop places when possible. The place I called said they had one room but that it would not be ready until 8 p.m. That was very odd, and it set off an alarm in me, but I wasn't going to get there much before dark anyway. When I arrived,

I had to wait a long while to get into my room. I had the feeling that maybe they had to kick a relative out so that they could get my rent money. It was small and adequate, and I didn't really much mind the wad of hair that they had missed on the bathroom wall. I know a lot of people who would have been mortified to stay there. All my third-world country travel had prepared me for this. This was a palace compared to many places I had stayed in my travels. I slept very well.

48 miles.

On Day 5, I traveled on back roads through Quincy and Gretna. I did not have to get back on Highway 90 until Chattahoochee, Florida. That is where I crossed the Apalachicola River. This route was beautiful and wet. There were a lot of creeks and rivers draining Georgia. The Apalachicola River marks the crossing of my first time zone this trip.

The day felt long, and I had had enough biking for the day about five miles past Grand Ridge. I broke one of my rules and pushed the bike through an old rusted-open gate past a rusty old "no trespassing" sign. I told myself that they didn't really mean it and spent the night at the edge of a woods next to a newly plowed field. It was a beautiful, quiet spot. A good stealth camp is a joy.

42 miles.

Breakfast is my favorite meal, and I was in easy range of a breakfast in Marianna, Florida. In the past I camped too far from the next town and could not get there before they had stopped serving breakfast.

I did not choose well this time when I stopped at a small diner on the outskirts of town. Although I carry a 10-foot charging cord, they did not have any place I could plug in my phone. Being stationary for that long without charging a device felt wasteful. On top of that, the breakfast was nothing to boast about. I was mostly finished with my breakfast when a distinctive odor of ozone arose from an electrical fire. Something went wrong with the grill. As I was leaving, they were closing the store until they could get it worked out.

My phone-charging paradigm was failing. Soon I would turn north into Alabama, and I would ride off of my ACA paper map, making me dependent on GMB. That would use more juice.

Highway 90 to Cottondale was flat, and from Cottondale to Chipley it was perfectly straight and flat. It was open road—good for high-speed cruising.

I stopped at the Piggly Wiggly grocery store in Chipley and bought a bag of salad. Sometimes you can get salad "kits" that have other ingredients to mix in. Such was not the case this time. It was just a bag of mixed greens. The advantage to this was that I could eat the salad with my fingers as I rode—and I am all about riding.

Since I have always walked with a limp, my back has developed scoliosis. My spine is out of whack. Now, in my advanced age, it has left me with an inability to stand for any length of time—not even a minute. I can lean against something for a very short time, and then I must sit down. If I cannot sit, then I must eat on the move. Because of this, when I become the benevolent dictator of the world (BDW), I will promulgate that a bench be put in front of every grocery and convenience store or gas station that serves food.

Just before Bonifay, I lucked into a special stop. There was a Kingdom Hall that had a wonderful, shaded breezeway out front and... a working power outlet!!! I rolled out my ridge mat and lay down to luxuriate. I get that it might not sound extravagant, but a rest stop out of the Florida sun with a breeze and electricity is exactly that for me—luxury!

After a wonderful rest—recharging both myself and my phone batteries—the road awaited. I was overtaken by two bicycle travelers at the same time. We had a nice chat. One guy was from Tallahassee heading for Pensacola. The other was on a very ambitious journey traveling from Massachusetts to Jacksonville, Florida to Natchez, Mississippi and then up the Natchez Trace and back to Mass. At this point I was just telling people I was headed for Jackson, Mississippi. It was early in the trip, and it sounded ludicrous to say I was headed for Seattle. I envied the guy who was going to do the Natchez Trace. I had driven parts of it before. It is a 440-mile road that angles northeast across Mississippi and into Tennessee. The speed limit is only 50 MPH, which keeps the big-hurry motorists off. Commercial vehicles are not allowed, making it an awesome bicycle route.

Towards nightfall, I ensconced myself in a woodsy hidey-hole near Argyle, Florida. I wanted to stop short of DeFuniak Springs because I needed a few things there (including breakfast) before turning north into Alabama.

61 miles.

On the morning of Day 7, my weather app predicted that three days of rain were likely. I was despairing a little, and I dragged into DeFuniak Springs in a funk. I was outfitted to ride in the rain, but I didn't want to. Riding a bike in the rain is dicier with slipping potential, and there is less stopping power with rim brakes. And visibility is hampered for drivers. Even if the windshield wipers are working, there are no wipers on side windows. Extra caution is required if you are encountering an automobile where the driver is seeing you (or not) out of a side window. And people are usually in the same hurry even if conditions have deteriorated.

The feeling of wanting to quit was haunting me again, and I encountered an unfortunate situation that I had not anticipated. Until now, most of my distance biking was carried out under the wise, kindhearted guidance of Adventure Cycling Association maps. Now that I needed actual paper maps, there were none to be found. For most of my life, you could go into any gas station and find many state and local maps. It had been a given. With the advent and onslaught of cell phone and GPS capabilities, paper maps (again, like myself) had become a thing of the past. Even the Walmart didn't have any. I couldn't use a road atlas because the state maps are not detailed enough for bicycle travel. I especially needed one in case my cell phone died. If that happened, I would barely be able to figure out where I was, much less how to go on.

Okay. Rain in the forecast. No map. Wanting to quit. Instead, I put the pedal to the metal, so to speak, and headed into Alabama. The first town just past the border is Florala. It has an interesting layout. Highway 55 turns into a double wide street called Main Street. I stopped on the sidewalk to get a feel for what I wanted to do. I wasn't hungry, but a coffee sounded good. I had barely stopped when a fellow came out to chat me up. He seemed like a nice guy and knew everything about Florala and the surrounding area. He even offered to put me up in the travel trailer in his yard if I wanted to stop.

It was too early in the day for me to settle in. We talked for a bit and then I asked him about the best coffee in town. He directed me about a half block away to his son's coffee shop. I got an excellent iced Americano to go and got back on the highway.

I was really jazzed by my coffee, and I took Google Maps Bicycle's (GMB) recommendation on some back roads to get to Andalusia. That is when I discovered that GMB assumes you have a mountain or gravel bike. It blithely directs you down unpaved roads of varying quality. Although they were good firm roads, it made me wish there was some way to filter for paved roads. If it had been wet, the going might not have been so good. But the roads were nice, dry, and quiet.

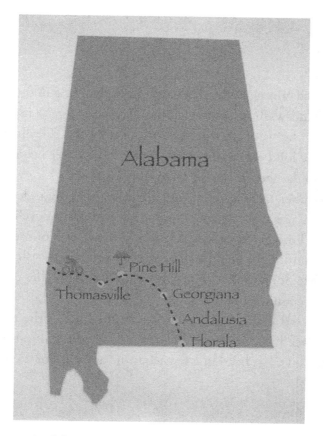

I rolled into Andalusia under a serious threat of rain. My radar app indicated no escape, so I decided to get a motel room. I had really covered some ground and thought an indoor bed would lend itself to a nice recuperation. Once again, I chose poorly. The room and bed were good enough, but the people in the adjacent room—seemingly a large, resident family—were extremely noisy. They had to communicate with each other over a loud television I could hear clearly. This went on late into the night and started again astonishingly early in the morning. My highway earplugs made it barely tolerable.

77 miles.

It had started raining in the night and was still raining in the morning. I always hand-wash my biking clothes whenever I get a motel room. I often dry the wash on the back of the bike as I ride. In this case running the loud air conditioner all night as a dryer helped dry my clothes and dampen the noise from the neighbors.

The weather radar app indicated that it was going to let up soon. My laundry was dry enough. I only pack two pair of cycling shorts, two bright lime-green cycling shirts, and three pairs of socks. I wear one outfit until I get in a situation where I can hand-wash it and put on the other. Sometimes that is many days, but that is life on the road for the impecunious.

Whenever I get a motel room, I take the bike in the room with me. No place has ever cared. I always ask for the ground floor, but my loaded bike has been in a few elevators as well. For me, stairs are not navigable.

CHAPTER 6

The Tempest

Cheap motel rooms are often dark as was the case here. But this time it led to a critical accident. My bike was loaded up, and I was ready to go. I was looking around for my glasses. They are wire-framed, and sometimes I have trouble finding them in good light. This room had cave lighting. As I walked around the bed, I heard and felt the most sickening crunch.

I was afraid to look. I realized that I had flipped my glasses off the bed and onto the floor. This wasn't just a little bent-frame circumstance. It was a full-on, crushed-flat-to-the-floor situation. "Dang," I thought. "I should have brought my spare pair." (No shit!) I was somewhat relieved to find the lenses still intact except for one small chip out of a corner. I checked the map app to see if there was a Walmart in Andalusia. I had purchased this pair with titanium frames in a Walmart back in Gainesville, Florida. Luckily, there was a Walmart about three miles away. I vacated the room and rode there in the diminishing rain.

They had the frame I needed, and, even more, they had the optician I needed. He was patient and determined to help me get back on the road. Patience was key because the screws in the frame were corroded shut from age. The only way to get the lenses out of the titanium frames was to file the frames off, and it took a very long time. In the meantime, I shopped for ingredients for my dog-repellant bottle. It goes fast. In the southern states I had probably been averaging two or three dog chases per day.

The optician was successful, and I was ecstatic to have a critical issue resolved quickly. I tried to tip him ten bucks, but he said it was not allowed and that he was happy to help. I thanked him profusely, and my new glasses frames and I got back on the road. By then, the rain had temporarily stopped.

Getting out of Andalusia remained challenging as I had to leave via a very busy four-lane road with a long upward grade and crappy shoulder. I was happy to finally get to relax on County 107 AKA Sunnyside Street. A little later, I stopped at a Dollar General outside of McKenzie, Alabama. When coffee is otherwise unavailable, I will grab a cold, canned coffee at a convenience store.

I was leaned up against the wall (no bench) at the side of the building, and two women came over to ask about my trip. I was still saying that I was headed to Jackson, Mississippi, but I added that I might go on to Denver after that. They asked a few more questions about distance biking, and then one of them handed me a $20 bill. She said she hoped it helped, and they left. Such a beautiful example of open-handed generosity!

I got back on Alabama 55 and took it to Georgiana. There was the continuing threat of rain, so I stopped there because I found a church that had a carport-like awning I could set my tent under. As usual I hoped no one would care.

40 miles.

Day 9 started with decent gas station coffee just a few miles from my campsite. I crossed under Interstate 65. It was cloudy, but the rain predicted for last night had not materialized. It looked like it could go either way for rain today. I traveled on Route 7 through Butler

Springs and then turned onto Alabama 10 toward Pine Apple, Alabama. Just outside of town, I got caught in a sudden, heavy downpour. I didn't have time to take shelter or get my rain gear on. I got quite wet, and then it was over. I wasn't terribly uncomfortable because the temperature was about 72 degrees. I just kept going until arriving at a teeny town called Oak Hill—not that there was much to Pine Apple. However, Oak Hill had an old-time, wooden country store replete with benches! I rolled up to the three people sitting on the benches, and they did not hesitate to invite me to join them. I went inside and bought two delicious barbecue sandwiches and enjoyed them on the benches with my new pals. We had as relaxed and comfortable a conversation as could be had with complete strangers. I was probably there an hour. They were happy to tell me how crazy it was to ride a bike long distance, and I was happy to say that it was a great way to meet people like them. One of the men had traveled a lot in the United States for work, and we compared notes on other places. As I was getting ready to roll away, one of them grabbed two bottled waters out of his truck and gave them to me. More open-handed generosity.

The weather radar showed that rain was going to be a sure thing this evening. I hurried to Camden and then raced along Alabama 10 to Alabama 5. Darkness was closing in, and I was hoping to find shelter. This was going to be a real storm, promising high winds and heavy rains. I rode through town, but there were no motels and no good shelter areas. I would not find out until the next day that there were some pretty good spots just a little further on. The problem was that I was already a couple miles off my route and did not want to get farther off it.

I rode back up 5 past Mike's Country Kitchen—a restaurant that looked promising for breakfast. I pulled into a parking area for logging truck trailers. There was nothing good about it. It had a gritty caliche-like surface. It was almost completely dark when I got set up next to

one of the trailers. Putting my rainfly on was hope against hope.
72 miles.

The night was loud. Much louder than my motel room back in Andalusia. The wind howled. Thunder and lightning were continuous—the rain prodigious. What a storm! Turbulence! Tumult! …in a tent! Tornados? The rainfly only slowed the rain down coming through my wind-battered tent. I'm not sure when in the night the rivulet from the parking area made its way across my tent floor.

On Day 10, 500 miles from home, I woke up in a soggy bag of wet feathers. Not that I slept much. It was sprinkling lightly outside and heavily overcast. The weather radar showed that the storm had mostly passed. Everything I had that was not sealed in a waterproof pannier was soaked. I was only chilled, right at the edge of being uncomfortably cold. The wet feathers did not help at all. I lay there thinking how much nicer it would be to be sitting at Mike's Country Kitchen having a warm breakfast, but I was not ready to break my saturated camp. I looked on my phone to see if there were any laundromats nearby. The phone showed none. I looked to see if Mike's was open yet. It was!

I dug out my dry biking outfit and my raincoat and bolted for Mike's, leaving my campsite as it was. At this point I felt that if anyone stumbled upon my camp and took everything, I would be grateful. Then I would be able to emancipate myself from this lunatic odyssey.

Mike's was pretty busy, and people kept coming in. It turns out that electricity was out in many places around the area. Many other people besides myself were grateful that Mike's had electricity and breakfast. The mood was cheerful. I think everyone was happy that the violent storm did not produce any tornados. I was especially glad about that having been ensconced outside in a tent. I thought about the possibility of a tornado during the maelstrom, but I am lucky in that where I can do nothing, a feeling of resignation takes over instead of panic. The eye of the mental storm. I had an intense learning experience with panic up in Alaska, but I'll get to that.

At the restaurant the patrons were convivial. I enjoyed conversing. Several people, when they found out my plight, said that I would be welcome to dry my stuff at their house but that they didn't have electricity due to the power outages. My nearest option for a laundromat was in Thomasville, 12 miles off my route.

Well-fed and coffeed, I went back and broke camp. My dense sleeping bag, which could have been weighed in ounces before, could now be weighed in pounds. My paperback book, *Zen and the Art of Motorcycle Maintenance*, was a soggy brick. I wrung things out as best I could and packed the bike. The load was quite a bit heavier than before. I set out on Alabama 5 for Thomasville. GMB indicated a possible back road, but I did not want to risk more hills than necessary, and I did not need to add mud to my list of tribulations.

CHAPTER 7

Crashing the Gate

When I lived on Kodiak Island in Alaska, I spent a lot of time in the bush. The cannery I worked at sat on the water at the base of a steep mountain. It was 80 miles from town by water, and there were no roads. The nearest humans to the cannery lived at West Point Village, a loose smattering of houses seven miles away. Uganik Bay where the facility was located was fjord-like, so hiking was always strenuous, and the chances of running into a brown bear were very high. The chances of running into another human—nil. You traveled by water or float plane or not at all. I had good friends who lived in a cabin around the corner in Mush Bay another seven miles past the village. One October they were taking a trip to Hawaii and asked me to housesit. I leaped at the chance. Except for two dogs, two cats, and some chickens, I would be alone for three weeks.

We tend to make our lives worse just with our minds. Alone does not equal lonely. Alone is a situation—lonely is a state of mind. Lonely is a problem we foist upon ourselves. We literally think ourselves into it. Our lives become better as soon as we realize that we do this to ourselves.

I try to catch myself when I call a situation a problem. The drowned camp in Alabama was a great lesson for me. When you think of something as a problem, the mind seems happy to expand on it ad nauseam. "Poor me, everything is soaked. Why did I take this trip?

I could have been killed; OMG, 12 extra miles; my book is ruined." All these things have truth to them, but the negative connotation automatically adds some heavy lifting in the thought stream that is completely, and utterly, unnecessary. It is a tempest inside. Watch your own mind and you will likely see this happening all the time. I would get more practice on this as the trip rolled on.

During the house-sitting gig in Alaska, I got myself into a weird situation that rapidly turned ugly. A windstorm swept in for a couple days that was quite nice. It was agreeable because the sky was only partly cloudy, and it wasn't raining. Alaska is beautiful at every turn, but when people were talking about visiting me in Kodiak, I would tell them, "Bring your raincoat and lots of money." At the point of this story, however, I was happy to not need the raincoat or money. 80 miles from town, money is all but useless. Well, maybe you could build a fire with it.

My friend's house was in the back of a little bight in the bay. The wind was blowing about 50 MPH across the front of the cove. Not that unusual in Alaska. Everything was fine.

I came from the back of the property and found the canoe swamped in the surge on the beach. The paddles that I had left in it were bobbing in the waves and headed out to sea.

As I mentioned, quiet transportation has always been one of my loves, and I have had a lot of canoeing experience. Not the least of which was a 100-mile trip through the Everglades. I might consider myself an expert except that what expert would leave a canoe to swamp on the beach? Add to that lapse in judgment that I decided to go after the paddles.

I rushed down the beach and grabbed the paddle out of the Sportyak. A Sportyak is basically a plastic bathtub meant to be paddled around on a mill pond. The paddle was about three-and-a-half feet long and in no way meant for paddling a canoe—especially not under these conditions. Nevertheless, I dumped the water out of the canoe and launched.

The wind was blowing across the bight, so I was able to get a long way—far enough to find myself in real peril. With the wind blowing across the front of the canoe and the small paddle, I was only able to go in a straight line, which meant further into danger. I had completely given up on the paddles and was trying to figure out whether I could back up or not, or if I could safely turn around. I did not get much time to think about it as a gust of wind picked up the bow of my little vessel and dumped me upside down.

For a long second, it was surreal. I was sinking in the clear bay water, looking up at an upside-down canoe and a blue sky dotted with white clouds. I clawed my way to the surface.

It was a plastic canoe without any extra flotation, so it only stayed at the surface. I could not use it for anything except a modicum of support. If I tried to use it to hold myself up, it sank.

The water was cold—the low 50s at best. I automatically pushed away from the canoe to start my swim to shore but sank straight down.

I thrashed my way back to the surface and rested my hand on the canoe. I wasn't going anywhere. I had way too much clothing on, and my rubber boots added too much drag. When I looked back to gauge my distance from shore, I was sickened. I knew I couldn't make it, and panic started to crash the gate on my sanity. I could feel panic rising in my body. I felt constriction in my abdomen and chest that rose steadily up my neck. Then it rose into my face. I was about to lose it.

Luckily for me, somehow, calm consciousness took over. I don't know why, and I cannot take credit for it. The constricting panic stopped at my cheeks. I could feel them flush, and then I felt them unflush. The sensation went back down the way it came. I was about to be overwhelmed by panic, but now I was quickly out of it. Once again, I was lucid… in as much as I ever am.

I looked back and saw the dog that I had let out of the house. She was walking nervously up and down the beach. I'm sure she was wondering what the hell I was doing swimming on a day like this.

I had two things going for me: I was a good swimmer, and I could hold my breath a very long time. I had not been a good student in grade school and middle school. Instead of paying attention in class, I watched the second hand on the clock as I held my breath. Without knowing I was doing myself any good at all, I was unwittingly building my vital capacity. These skills were further honed during years and years of snorkeling in Florida.

The cold was clearly going against me. The water was cold, and the air was cold, which was why—along with my other stupidities—I ended up in the water fully clothed. I even had my knee boots on.

I needed to get some of my gear off to have a chance of making it to shore. I let go of the canoe, and as I sank I worked at getting one of my rubber boots off. With a fierce struggle, I could only get it half off before having to slash my way back to the surface for air. With another sinking scramble, I was able to wrestle the boot the rest of the way off. I let it go to the bottom and fought my way back to oxygen.

It took two more tries to successfully get the other boot off. As I bobbed in the waves, I knew that wasn't going to be enough. I would still sink if I took my hand off the canoe. I had on a jean jacket that was fleece-lined, which would be at the top of the list of the worst things to have on if you ended up in the water. It was the kind where when you pulled your arm out of the sleeve, the inner sleeve reversed out with it. I thought about Houdini and his legendary underwater tricks. But in my case, an insane challenge was thrust upon me by my own idiocy. Also, it was hugely ironic to be that cold and to be getting undressed.

Down I went again, certain that my life depended on getting my arm out of that heavy, waterlogged jacket sleeve in one try. It helped that I had gotten my boots off. I wasn't sinking quite as fast, and the boots weren't impeding my kicks. I succeeded and returned to the surface where I shook the jacket the rest of the way off.

With that, I was done disrobing. I still had fleece-lined jeans on, and I was still heavy in the water, but I could float very low without the canoe. I pushed away and started backstroking toward shore with the waves constantly washing over my nose.

Finally, I came to a skiff anchored offshore. At the bow I tried to pull myself up, but I was too frozen for any hope of that. There was no strength left in my arms. I hand-over-handed along the gunnel until I got to the outboard engine and tried to climb it. I had to use the up-and-down action caused by the boat tossing in the waves. Each time the stern kicked up, I got a little higher until I finally flopped into the motor well and then into the boat.

So cold was I. Sooo cold!

I pulled stiffly on the starting rope. This engine was renowned for not wanting to start. I pulled and pulled, but it wouldn't go. I had serious doubts that I could make it the rest of the way to shore if I got back in the water. But the other option was to freeze to death trying to start the engine. When there was almost nothing left of me, the engine fired, and I was able to motor to shore. The tide was falling, so I just left the boat at the shoreline and walked up the beach in my socks like a mummified zombie. As I progressed toward the warm house, I realized that my glasses had joined my boots and my jacket at the bottom of the bay.

When I got to the house, I stripped down and dried myself. There was hot water, but I was so cold that even tepid water felt like it was burning me. I draped myself in a sleeping bag and paced. I thought about my encounter with the near panic. What happened? It was clear to me that I was on the verge, but then somehow, I backed away from it. For me to say that "I" backed away from it felt like an exaggeration. I knew that I couldn't take credit for it. Something more essential was at play, and it is going to take the rest of this book for me to explore with you what I have discovered.

There is a pattern cyclists notice in smallish towns. You ride in on a two-lane road with some shoulder, but in town it will become four lanes with no shoulder. Sometimes there is a sidewalk to get you out of the traffic, but such was not the case in Thomasville, Alabama. Between entrances to the businesses, there were curbs and ditches. It would be extremely difficult for fit, agile pedestrians to navigate the side of the road in Thomasville, but it is practically impossible for cyclists. Unfortunately for everyone, it was very trafficky. I had to ride on the edge of the right lane, which made a lot of motorists extremely unhappy. Several people blared their horns—the unhappy motorist's answer to frustration. To give everyone a break, I pulled into a funeral home parking lot. Even after about 10 minutes standing there, a foursome of young men went past me and honked and flipped me off. Had they gone around the block to do that? Maybe they went around so that they could run me over and were disappointed that I had gotten out of the road.

This is a great example of how we create our own anguish. A driver comes upon some stupid dipstick riding his loaded bike in the road along the curb, and how the driver reacts to that can be a choice. Thankfully, most people will slow down a little and swerve around. They may think nothing of it. However, some will feel severely affronted. They are the ones that will blare their horns in righteous indignation or flip the cyclist off—or both. It is a mental illness born of ego, and I can attest to that because I used to be that way.

My father was an aggressive driver, and I learned from him. He likely learned that from his father. When I was young, just like these anxious people, I felt I was right. I could not see that I was creating this angst within myself and spreading it to others with my behavior. Back then I could not see that I had a choice. These people, and the younger Ken, believed that the cyclist, slow driver, construction zone, long red light, or whatever *caused* the unhappiness. But ALL that suffering is internal, self-generated, and completely unnecessary.

Anthony de Mello once said, "No event and no person on earth has the power to give you a negative feeling." By the time I heard that statement, I had matured enough to give him the benefit of the doubt and examine his proposition. I've since found it to be 100 percent true. If you allow yourself to unlearn these absurdities with which we have been inculcated, what remains of life will be happier than you could ever have imagined. There is nothing you need to believe in. It is experiential. You do not need to meditate, pray, or do any practices. You only need to observe your own reactions... to be aware. To that little list of petty stressors above the question is "So what?" and the tranquil, wise, world-improving answer is "So nothing."

It would have been nice if I had been taught to take all the small, daily inconveniences like those mentioned above and to make nothing of them. I managed to make something of those things without seeing that I was only hurting myself and others around me.

Having started down this road of self-realization one can lead into a happier, more loving life. I ruined my pants, spilled coffee on the carpet, and said something dumb. After any of those things, we sick people tell a commensurate story: the pants were expensive, that stain won't come out, I've embarrassed myself. We beat ourselves up unnecessarily. We do this with other people all the time also. It is possible and attenuating, and even healing, to—after any of the above remarks say—"So what... so nothing." Then we are much closer to facing a beautiful reality.

Within a few blocks, I was able to connect to a few back roads to get the rest of the way across town to the laundromat. Thank you, Google Maps Bicycle. This was among the worst main streets for biking that I would encounter. Absolutely terrible for cycling or walking.

The laundromat was large and spacious, so I wheeled my bike inside and started to unpack. The attendant lady came over and told me I couldn't bring my bike in. Shoot, there went a wonderful convenience. But before I could get packed back up to take it outside, she kindly acquiesced and admitted there was plenty of room. Don't you just love spontaneous compassion? It is a choice, and it is the beautiful choice.

It was late in the day when I finally got everything dry, and I was worn out. I took a room at the Relax Inn and did just that.

13 miles.

At first light on Day 11, I exited the Relax Inn and Thomasville, Alabama. It was a Sunday, and I was looking forward to light traffic. I was a little happy to be leaving this town behind, but the only place I could get coffee before I left was a gas station at the far edge of town. I was taking Highway 43. It would angle me toward Route 10, which I had left the night of the storm. It was not so terribly out of the way after all, and with no backtracking.

I went to the counter to pay for my coffee, and the attendant said, "Don't worry about it." Another free coffee for no reason that I could tell. A bit more spontaneous kindness. Again, the beautiful choice.

Traffic was indeed light. I sped along enjoying my recovery from disaster, but then ran into a setback in Butler, Alabama.

Occasionally, I would hit a town that was taking COVID more seriously than most, and this was one of them. I stopped at McDonald's because east of the Mississippi River, all the McDonald's restaurants that I had encountered had electric outlets in the dining area. This McDonald's, however, was not allowing people to sit inside. I rolled on to a Hardee's, and they were letting people dine inside, but they had no electric outlets. Jeez!

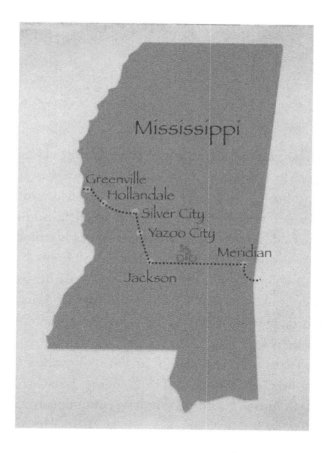

The Piggly Wiggly grocery store was a couple blocks further where I spied an empty electrical outlet outside. It was in-between two vending machines set apart in the shade. I parked there for a while and ate a bag of salad as I charged my phone and my spare battery.

Most people had masks on, which I had been finding very unusual. But passersby were curious and kindly, and I had a nice, social time there in my phone-charging cubbyhole. Once I was all charged up, I got back on Alabama 10 until I crossed the border into Mississippi. I found a very nice campsite in the woods and set up without need of the rainfly.

57 miles.

The morning of Day 12, I awoke fresh. I was getting close to Ken and Linda's house in Jackson, and I was looking forward to seeing them and getting a break. I had met Ken in Alaska at the Uganik Cannery four decades before. It was in my earlier years at the cannery, and he and I worked side by side at one of those relentlessly tedious jobs that are legion at a cannery. He was a student from Humbolt University in California trying to have adventure and increase his coffers. Back then, if they could take it, the salmon industry in Alaska provided income for many students. Like Ken, a lot of them were students at colleges on the West Coast of the continental states.

The next spring, I visited him at Humbolt when I was on a hitchhiking odyssey, returning to the cannery. I had a terrific time visiting him in Arcata, California, but it was one of many stops for me, and after that, we lost track of one another. An amazing coincidence brought us back together years later.

I broke camp and got back out on Alabama 10, which was now Mississippi 19. The luxurious, low-traffic, Sunday route had morphed into a racetrack for semi-trucks. A pleasurable, fast ride had turned into harrowing horror. The road shoulders in Alabama had those terrible rumble strips that make them unbikeable. I do not think that whoever came up with the idea of rumble strips had ever heard of a bicycle. Or perhaps they had never dreamed that anyone would ride a bike other than on a playground. Rumble strips done right are probably helpful, but the way they are often cut into the roads in Alabama, Mississippi, and Louisiana is nightmarish for cyclists. Sometimes they use the entire road shoulder and force bicycle riders into traffic. Then, even where the shoulder is extremely wide, they will cut the strip right down the center of it. It is difficult to ride on what is left of smooth pavement on the dirt side of the shoulder, and one risks going into the ditch. So again, the cyclist is impelled to ride on the traffic side. Presumably, these rumble strips are meant to warn inattentive drivers that they are going off the road. I really do not understand cutting them through the middle of the shoulder. Is that to alert the driver that they are already off the road? Whenever I ride past a highway department office, I want to go inside and say, "Half as deep, half as wide and cut them into the white line." That would be enough to keep all but the drunkest of motorists out of the ditches.

In Mississippi they don't seem to bother much with road shoulders at all. It is said to be the poorest state. Perhaps they cannot afford the extra pavement. This teeny shoulder barely kept me out of the lane with the trucks. I wasn't certain I could survive it very long. GMB indicated that the next chance I had to get off was Highway 514. It took me out of my way, but it was life or death at this point. The turnoff was only a couple of miles after my campsite, but my nerves were frazzled by the time I got there.

I pulled off the highway with such a feeling of gratitude. It was a beautiful neighborhood, and within a few blocks, the cacophony turned into tranquility. The road was nice and flat, and I could hear birds singing. Idyllic. It was called Shannon Road.

I was low on water, and there was no indication that I was going to find any for a long time. Eventually, I passed through an intersection where a man was working in his yard close to the road. I rang my bell in a greeting, and he waved and gestured to me to stop. When people see me on this loaded bicycle, they often are curious about where I have come from and where I'm going. Such was the case. He was an avid cyclist himself but had not done overnight trips. As we were parting, I asked him if he knew somewhere I could get water. He invited me over to his shop and topped me off. He even had ice!

At this time of year in Mississippi, mid-April, the nights are cool, but the days can be quite hot. He warned me that although it was flat terrain here, this route toward Jackson was very hilly.

I stayed on 514 for miles, and the elevation changes got progressively worse. The road crossed one creek after another, and I found myself having to push the bike to the top of many short hills. The weather was cloudless and warm. By the time I got to Energy, Mississippi, I was low on energy. But I felt like I had to keep going.

There was nothing in Middleton, Mississippi except the Shady Grove Church. It had a nice grassy lawn, and I had had enough. I pulled off and stretched my mat out in some shade and had a beautiful hour nap.

I got up feeling revived, but I knew I didn't want to go to Jackson on this route. The creeks were running north to south. Heading west meant that the road was going to continue dropping into every creek bottom and then climbing back out. I decided to head north toward Meridian because I needed to be between the creeks instead of crossing them. I chose to take Clarke County Road 450. It was eventually going to put me on another arterial highway, but hopefully, it would have a better shoulder and less traffic. That is always the hope. This road was still hilly, but they were inclines I could top without having to get off the bike.

When I got to Alabama 145, I found that it pretty much paralleled US Route 45 to Meridian. This is a good biking situation because the larger US road takes a lot of the traffic off the smaller highway.

Either Meridian is a very diminished town or GMB just took me through the poorest part of it. A lot of dead industry and indigent neighborhoods. I was led out of town on Fifth Street, which bled into Old Highway 80—an awesome road for biking. I traveled on it many miles before coming upon a "Road Closed Ahead" sign. A few cars had passed me, so I thought I would encounter a road blockage situation that I could walk my bicycle around.

I traveled several more miles to a very broken bridge. I don't know where those cars had gone, but they had certainly not crossed the creek here. The replacement bridge spanned a small creek that had evidently flooded and washed the old bridge out. It smelled like the flood had also taken out a sewer lift station. But the event was not new. I wondered why GMB didn't know to warn me about it. Fortunately for me, they had started repairing the bridge. There were two huge cement slabs crossing the creek with a big drop on both ends of them. I dismantled my load and lifted the bike and the panniers separately up onto the slabs. I walked my stuff across and down the other end and reassembled. Anything to avoid that giant backtrack. It would have been at least 20 extra miles.

I was back on Old Highway 80 and would be on it all the way to Brandon, Mississippi. It paralleled Interstate 20, so there was the beautiful effect that most of the traffic heading east and west was on the Interstate. Old Highway 80 was a mostly straight, mostly flat blessing. The only drawback was that most of the businesses along the route had perished. I stopped at one very dingy convenience store that had a little kitchen serving food to go. It was dismal out front and depressing inside. I do not suffer from mysophobia, but I went to use the restroom and encountered pure destitution. All their cleaning equipment was strewn around in there (possibly unused). The tiny room was filthy, the toilet had a big chip out of it, and there was no running water at the sink. Oh yeah… and no sign telling employees that they must wash their hands before returning to work. It was squalid! I looked around the dingy store and elected to dine elsewhere.

GMB indicated a restaurant option a few miles down the road, but the diner turned out to be long dead. Such is the life of the XC cyclist.

It was getting time to camp, and somewhere past Chunky, Mississippi, I turned off on a road that indicated a church nearby. I found the church and walked around back to see if it was suitable for a stealth camp. To my chagrin, I could see a neighboring house through the brush. But it was starting to get dark, so I broke one of my rules and set up my tent regardless. The day felt very long, though I had not made that much distance. It was a gorgeous, cool night, and I slept well.

42 miles.

On Day 13, I woke up very early. I broke camp and hit the road at first light. There was a giant weather front coming, and rain would not be avoided. The radar image looked like the one that had flooded me out back in Pine Hill, Alabama. I wondered if I could make it to Ken and Linda's house. They live in Brandon, which is east of Jackson, so that was a little closer. I can be tenacious at staying in the saddle when motivated, and this impending storm was highly motivating. Making it to Brandon would be the difference between being in a dry house and being in my tent through another deluge.

I rode like heck, never assuming that I could make it. Old Highway 80 stayed true. The grades were long and shallow. The traffic was light. Through the towns of Hickory, Newton, and Forest, I hardly slowed down. Forest even had a Walmart, but I could not think of anything I needed more than to get to Brandon.

Just before Pelahatchie, Old Highway 80 merged into New Highway 80. I was getting closer to the urban area, and traffic was picking up. So were the grades. 80 was losing its charm, but I was getting close to my salvation destination. I had no idea where their house was, but of course GMB knew exactly where it was—and it knew a back way for getting there. Just as the traffic situation was getting ugly, GMB took me off 80 and onto Paige McDill Road. The back route felt circuitous, but I joyfully arrived at Ken and Linda's house about an hour before dark.

70 miles.

Ken and I had lost touch and managed to reconnect in a most unusual way. The last time I had seen him was in 1981 when I hitchhiked through Eureka, California, and he was at Humbolt. After that, we had no more contact. Eight years later, I was still working at the cannery in the summers, but I was attending the University of Florida in the winter. As soon as classes ended, I would head back to the cannery in Uganik Bay to make some jing. I had a roommate at UF who was a most excellent friend who had been an employee when I was a McDonald's manager in Sarasota, Florida back in 1972. Brad was another long-term contact of mine. The same Brad who offered to rescue me on this trip if I needed it.

While I was away in Alaska, a classmate of Brad's asked him if he wanted to go birding and would he mind if she brought her boyfriend along. During their conversations, Brad mentioned that his roommate was up in Kodiak, Alaska. Her boyfriend, Ken, said that he had worked at a cannery in Kodiak. It turns out that this was my old pal and workmate from the cannery. He and his girlfriend were attending the University of Florida. What a way to discover that! An amazing irony.

Ken and Linda seemed pleased to see me. COVID was center stage, and the media hype seemed to be doing more harm than good. I was at least hoping that they would let me set my tent up in the yard where I would have access to a dryer. As it was, they let me stay in their house and let my bike stay in the garage. Both were excellent luxuries. I was able to spread all the stuff out of my panniers over the garage floor and sort out what was needed and what wasn't. I decided by now to continue to Denver. I was over the hump.

I had written to Venture 4th about my lifetime-guaranteed, leaking, self-inflating sleeping pad. They had apologized and asked me where they could send a replacement. A new inflatable mat had already arrived. Venture 4th embodies commendable integrity.

I desperately needed to improve my phone-charging capacity. I had ordered another solar-charged battery to be sent to K&L's house, and it was also there. It was larger than my first one, and it barely fit on my handlebar rack. It was also twice as heavy. Hopefully, it would work better. It is rare for me to go up a long grade without cogitating on what I could get rid of. Now I had added weight.

If my phone had died anywhere on those back roads of Alabama and Mississippi, I would have been screwed. While in Jackson, I needed to hunt down paper maps of my next states. I needed maps of Mississippi, Arkansas, Oklahoma, Kansas, and Colorado. The maps I could not get in bookstores I would have to order online and hope they got to me before I left.

I also had to wash my sleeping bag. It got drowned in Pine Hill and dried in Thomasville, but it had not been washed. It was... let's say... unpleasant-smelling.

It rained torrentially the night I arrived and then rained a few more times before I left. I got to spend all that rain time indoors. Fantastic!

I broke another rule at Ken and Linda's. I normally would not stay more than three days, but I stayed there five. It is their fault. They made me feel welcome. I was able to get all my needs met, and I was even treated to a couple trips out on the Ross Barnett Reservoir in their boat.

I found most of the maps I needed around town and only had to order one. I sat on Ken and Linda's kitchen floor and cut them up, saving only the parts I thought I would use. It probably sounds like a desperate measure for saving weight, but why not? Every little bit helps.

About the time they probably thought I had moved in to stay, I left. Day 18 was a Sunday, and that is the best day to exit a city. As early as possible is also best. Right at first safe light, I rolled out of their garage and back into my odyssey.

Like most large towns, Jackson has some excellent bike paths. GMB is indispensable for getting through towns and cities. It kept me on bike paths and decent roads. They were especially decent due to light traffic. At the town of Flora, I had to get on US 49, which wasn't terrible even though the road conditions were. It is a four-lane divided highway with **NO** shoulder. None! I had to ride in the right lane for more than 20 miles. It was straight and wide open, so I could watch the traffic in my rearview mirror ease into the left lane as needed. Occasionally, there would be too many vehicles in a traffic cell for a truck to be able to get over, and I would have to endure a close squeeze. There actually is enough room—it just doesn't feel like it. Any amount of shoulder would help, but Mississippi did not provide that. After all, it wasn't customary in that state.

I got off at Yazoo City and ate at a Wendy's. They allowed people to sit indoors there. It was nice to sit on something besides a bicycle seat after 52 miles without hardly stopping. The wind had been about five MPH in my face most of the time. When I dropped down into the "Delta" on 49W, also a four-lane divided highway, the wind came up to nine MPH and was head-on. I got off 49W at Gooden Lake Road and within a mile or two came upon a little church that was not far from some giant agricultural industry buildings. I think it was a cotton gin. I set up my tent behind the tiny church next to their tiny cemetery and enjoyed a gorgeous sunset on the Delta and a clear, starry night.

73 miles.

On the morning of Day 19, I was treated to a fantastic sunrise. Most of the Delta is flat and wide open. I had dropped down a hill back in Yazoo City, and I would not hit another hill until Pine Bluff, Arkansas. The only rises would be bridges over water courses or railroads. I was excited to be in range of the Mississippi River. I had crossed it once before by bicycle. On my first trip, I crossed at New Roads, Louisiana. It is a very pleasing milestone to cross the river, especially for the second time. This time I would be crossing at Greenville, Mississippi.

On a bicycle trip, there can be a big difference between the time you expect to get somewhere and the time you actually arrive. Even if you don't think there is anything in the way.

GMB is cool because if you ask it for a route, say Jackson to Greenville, it will give you a blue route and often one or two alternates in gray. When you get to Wazoo City, you can ask it again about getting to Greenville and sometimes get a new main route and two new alternates. They look like options for adventure. Back in Alabama I used it and was put on some dicey roads for a touring bike, but it always worked. Today I would find out how wrong it could go.

CHAPTER 8

Lost in the Delta

I was cruising down Route 12, which was a no-shoulder two-lane road with a little too much traffic for my taste. GMB was showing me a nifty-looking shortcut to get over to the town of Arcola. It promised not to be trafficky by the looks of it. And indeed, it wasn't.

I got off 12 where GMB ushered me onto a dirt road that was plenty firm enough to navigate with Truckee. After a mile or so, it made a predicted curve, but the road degraded a little. I stopped for a snack and took stock of my water supply. In the more populated states, my three liters usually proved plenty. In fact, I rarely had to get into my third liter. When I had used up my first two, I always took the next opportunity to top off. This formula had worked up until today. I wasn't exactly overflowing with water, but Arcola was not that far away... at least not as the vulture flies.

After a few miles, the road became a dried mud track for giant tractors with the deep tread on their tires. It was horrible. Forward progress was extremely slow and extremely uncomfortable. There was no chance to avoid the giant succession of potholes caused by the tractor tires. My penchant not to backtrack was in question. But there's a certain hopefulness that takes over when I start to doubt this way. There were woods up ahead that might lead to a better road.

Hoo Boy! The road turned into a grass track that looked like it had not been used in months. Still, I was very close to the waterway that I would cross and possibly get into better terrain. I did not know it at the time, but I had entered the Holt Collier National Wildlife Refuge. Within about a half a mile, I came to a rusty "Road Closed" sign that was so enshrouded by bramble that I could hardly make it out. I left Truckee for a bit and crawled through the brush to see what the bridge looked like. There was about a 12-foot deep, muddy ditch and no clear sign that there had ever been a bridge. My heart sank at least as deep as that muddy trench.

I scrambled back to my bike and surveyed my water supply. Now it was critical. GMB was no help. It kept insisting on crossing the nonexistent bridge. I was on my last liter, and I drank a third of it. I was hoping to find an alternate route out of there soon, but now I would have to start rationing. I knew which direction I had to go to get back out on 12. I was trying to avoid backtracking over the horror route I had come in on. There was a cut through the forest that looked like it had been mowed in the last decade, so I followed it for a while. There was no indication that it was going to lead me out, and it was damp enough that my rear wheel would spin at times. I had to give up on it.

That meant going back over the hell route in the open until I came to a dirt rut road I had noticed earlier. It was hot and sunny, and I sipped my water until it was gone. I came to the mystery road and took it. It pointed in the correct direction, but there was no indication of it having been traveled very much. After a mile or two, I found out why.

I came upon a "Bridge Closed" sign. As far as I could see, I couldn't see anything. But what was left of this bridge was crossable with some effort. Route 12 had to be within two or three (or four or five) miles, and I would have to travel much farther than that if I were to backtrack all the way out.

I pushed the bike across the bridge and pedaled. Yes, I thought it was possible that I would come to a closed bridge that I couldn't cross. If that was the case, I would have to drink muddy water filtered through my biking shorts... or something.

Parched and exhausted, I finally came to the paved road. GMB was happy to tell me that I was about six miles away from Hollandale. Suddenly, I had the freedom of only one clear choice, and I rode to town. I found an air-conditioned restaurant and ordered a big meal with lots of water. What a relief! I stayed in the air conditioning until I was completely cooled, rested, and hydrated. I realized that although I had wasted hours being lost on my "shortcut," I could probably still make it across the Mississippi River before nightfall.

I left Hollandale refreshed and rode as if I had regained my youth. It felt like I had dodged a bullet, and now I would ride like one. I took Old Highway 61 north to Arcola and then zigzagged up to Highway 278. I crossed the Mississippi on the Greenville Bridge about an hour before sunset.

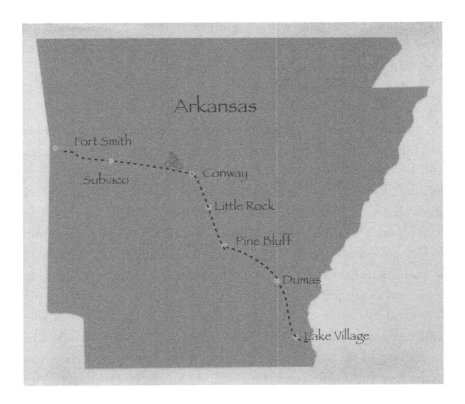

My first night in Arkansas was delightful. I pretty much chose the first building I came across and hid behind it. It was a small church. Something further off the highway would have been better, but it was too late to be choosey, and there was nothing else around. It looked like someone else had used the place for this purpose, and I cleaned up their mess before retiring to my tent. I was happy to know that there would be lots of services 10 miles away in Lake Village.

59 miles.

I woke up refreshed to a lovely sunrise and felt back in the groove. There was nothing to do but head north toward Pine Bluff on Scenic Highway 65. No getting lost today. The wind was WSW at about nine MPH. It was nice to have that slightly behind me. I did not find the ideal diner in Lake Village, so I had breakfast at McDonald's. At least they had electric outlets and a decent Americano.

In McGehee I stopped for a break at a convenience store/gas station. As usual there were no benches, so I was sitting on the cement against the wall next to my bike. A lovely young woman was putting gas in her car, but she kept looking over at me. Her many glances were obvious, and I wondered what that was about. When she was through filling her car, she walked straight toward me. She asked me if I was OK. I think that since I was sitting on the pavement, she might have thought I was homeless. I told her I was fine, but that did not stop her from handing me a $10 bill. She said, "Have a blessed day." As she turned to go back to her car, I heard myself tell her that she was beautiful in more ways than just one.

I tried to continue past Dumas, but the wind switched suddenly and came up to 20 miles an hour straight in my face. It was like someone had turned on a wind tunnel. I don't have the strength to pedal against 20 MPH, so I rode around Dumas for a while trying to find a suitable stealth camp. Nothing presented itself. I looked at all the churches, but there was no place to hide among them. I finally rode out of town to the west and found a very unsuitable hideout behind a parked semitruck with huge plastic tanks strapped on it. The straps squished the tanks where they crossed them. I wondered what was in them. God knows the kinds of chemicals they have out in these agricultural areas. But once again, desperation was setting in. There were no apparent leaks, so I set up my tent.

60 miles.

Yesterday evening's wind ushered in a cold front. Day 21 started out cold. I broke camp behind the semitruck in 37 degrees. It was one of those stealth camps that I was in a hurry to leave. I didn't want someone to show up for their truck full of whatever and find me. Most people are forgiving, but I didn't want to give anyone the choice to have to forgive me for trespassing.

I rode all the way to Pine Bluff with a cold, 11-MPH wind in my face. I kept my light riding jacket and long pants on all day. It had been flat, flat, flat, and the hills started up again right at Pine Bluff. Hence the name, I suppose. I found a nice coffee shop in town and had a terrific Americano and quiche. Not exactly dusty road kind of food, but I needed a lift to get me to push on. GMB let me down getting out of Pine Bluff. I was never sure what went wrong. Both of my map apps seemed confused, and GMB had me turning into a gated military site. Whoever was behind that fence was not so proud of it as to give it a name. It might have been the Pine Bluff Arsenal, or possibly the National Center for Toxicological Research—both were options. At any rate, I wanted nothing to do with either. I had to backtrack quite a way, and I got out by dead reckoning. It was weird that both map apps failed me at the same time.

I found a decent woodsy hole between Whitehall and Jefferson in an area with lots of houses around. A fenced-in dog spotted me as I turned up a little dirt road. He barked excitedly, and then, thankfully, he shut up. I could hear kids playing nearby as I set up my tent, but I was out of sight of anyone.

44 miles.

It was a pretty comfortable stealth camp. I stayed in my tent longer than usual because I didn't think I would be discovered, and it was only 39 degrees. As I departed my camp, it was amusing that the dog was clearly waiting for me to come out. He had his eye on the path, and as soon as he saw me, he started barking again. I told him he was a very good, attentive boy.

Down the road, there was a convenience store that looked a little dumpy from the outside, but I went in anyway. It was an all-metal building, and my phone would not work in there. Strava tracks me by satellite, and the building even knocked that out. I was served an excellent omelet and terrible coffee by a very friendly crew. I guess it is a hot spot if you are there at the right time. One woman asked if she could get a picture of me as one of her relatives was an XC cyclist.

After the photo op, I took Highway 365 all the way to Little Rock. It was a lovely ride that wound through both beautiful scenes and amazingly destitute areas. I was seeing livestock again. I had not seen any in the Delta.

There was almost no traffic on 365 because Interstate 530 had siphoned it all off. To go from Pine Bluff to Little Rock would take a car about 45 minutes on the Interstate. On this lovely back road, it would take a vehicle at least an hour and a half. There were very few automobiles. Besides, who, other than a cyclist, would want to subject themselves to the pockets of abject poverty sprinkled along this route?

Coming into Little Rock, I passed by the Bill and Hillary Clinton National Airport. Who knew there was such a thing?! I had to ride around in the city for a while because I had business to take care of. I had to receive and send documents which required a notary. It is a huge undertaking by bicycle. The last place I would have been able to do this would have been Jackson, Mississippi. You just don't come across those kinds of services easily while biking. As I said, for the most part, GMB is awesome for traversing cities.

Dropping down to the Arkansas River was impressive as was the beautiful pedestrian/bicycle bridge that crosses over the locks. A wonderful public resource.

Once I was north of the river, I found myself on 365 again and then on to Sturgis Road. Amazingly, after the perplexing, terrible road shoulder design (or lack thereof) on the roads in Alabama and Mississippi, Arkansas was a cyclist's dream. It was extremely rare to hit a road-shoulder situation that wasn't handled as if I had designed it myself. It was as though they anticipated that a bicyclist might actually use the roads! Where they felt they needed rumble strips, they were half as wide as in those other states and cut right into the white line at the side of the road. I rode all the way across Arkansas, and it was like that the entire way. Kudos to Arkansas!

Tonight's stealth camp was beautiful. I rode up a power line road and passed a turnoff for a huge construction project. There were woods and grass and no dwellings. From the looks of the weather radar, there would be rain tomorrow. I would get up early and race to Conway and get a motel room. It had been five days since my last shower. With luck I could get a room in a place that had a laundry room that was also near some supplies. With even better luck, the rain would stop, and I wouldn't have to spend two nights. For now, it was lovely here outside of Mayflower, Arkansas.

52 miles.

Day 23. I awoke to the rumble of a line of dump trucks coming up the power line road headed for the construction site. That was fine because I was excited to get to my next motel night. They had moved the rain forecast to evening, so I decided to race further on to Morrilton. Highway 64 was a breeze. It was another situation where Interstate 40 took most of the traffic away. I was working my way through Conway and got caught in an unanticipated cloudburst. I got quite wet before I pulled up to a two-story apartment building. I was standing outside an apartment window under the protection of the second-floor walkway. I looked at the radar image and could see that the rain was going to end in about 20 minutes. I imagined someone finding me stuck there and inviting me in for a cup of coffee and maybe even a Danish. One can dream. At least I didn't get discovered.

I left Conway and crossed the Arkansas River for the second time. This put me in, yes, Toad Suck, Arkansas. I was tempted to hang out there so I could tell people I bivouacked in Toad Suck, but instead I rolled on. I remember passing Toad Suck Harley Davidson.

I arrived at the Super 8 in Morrilton a little earlier than they prefer for check-in; however, when I rolled up on the bike, the front desk lady was very impressed to hear that I had ridden from Florida. I walked in with my cane, so she let me check in early and gave me a handicapped, ground-floor room. I had chosen this hotel because it had a laundry room. It also had a pool, but the pool was closed due to COVID.

Rain was pending, and I went out for an early dinner. Taco Bell was drive-through only, and Wendy's was not allowing inside seating. I had to do a restaurant upgrade to get to sit indoors. I was temporarily tired of the outdoors, so I dropped into Coulton's Steakhouse and Grill. I had excellent food and service there. I returned to my room at the Super 8 feeling so good! It was a badly needed and much-appreciated motel night. It stormed like hell all night. My tent and I and all my stuff stayed safely dry inside.

36 miles.

In the morning there was a break in the rain, but radar showed another squall coming. I decided to take a risk and ride over to the Kroger Supermarket to see what kind of meal or energy bars I might find. I didn't find anything suitable there and headed over to the Walmart across the street. I didn't like what they had either, but I had to get some anyway. I especially need them for low blood sugar events. They are a necessity even if they aren't the preferred quality. I checked my items out, but then found out that the only open restrooms were all the way in the back of the store. Even with my cane, that is a lot of hoofing for me.

When I came outside again, the rain was coming down in buckets. It is so dangerous to ride in that, but my warm room was only about a quarter mile away. I had taken all the panniers off in the room, so at least I was traveling light. I struck out into the torrent and got back to my room drenched. I had access to a warm shower, so I put my stuff in the dryer—again.

I stalled around waiting for the rain to end. They had decent, free coffee in the lobby, and the weather radar promised that it would be clear when this storm ended. There were no more squalls in the queue. I was granted a late checkout, and I went over to the Waffle House for breakfast and more lingering.

When I finally busted out of Morrilton, I was in the mood for motion. I was enjoying being back in the saddle. I crossed the Arkansas River again at Dardanelle and cruised Highway 22, a very enjoyable two-lane road that is far from the Interstate. I would now be south of the river until Fort Smith. I was pleased to be back in my tent again just after passing Delaware, Arkansas.

42 miles.

It was 48 degrees when I got up on Day 25. Highway 22 was a pleasure, and I eventually noted that it was in part because it was Sunday. I was blithely traveling down the road when I came upon an unexpected scene. First, I could hear church bells, but then, far across an open field dotted with Angus cattle, was a monstrous edifice. It looked like a cathedral. Of course, the bells ringing helped with that inference. Then I could hear chanting or singing faintly across the huge meadow.

In the town of Subiaco, I found out that it was a Benedictine Abbey. Who would have thought to put it there in backwater Arkansas—and in the late 1800s! Somebody hauled a lot of stone by horse and wagon to make this incongruous structure. I further learned that the abbey had donated 80 acres to form the town of Subiaco. The name is taken from the town in Italy where Saint Benedict founded his first monastery. I absorbed a little more of its Sunday magic and then rolled on.

Highway 22 was an excellent road for me without a lot of elevation changes. In fact, all of Arkansas felt good to me. In a large part that was because I didn't have to fight the previous two states' road shoulder designs. Plus, I didn't get too horribly lost like I did in Mississippi. I hit Fort Smith late in the afternoon and I had to cross the Arkansas River again to get into Oklahoma.

My introduction to Oklahoma was impressive, but not in a good way. It was flat, which was OK (get it?), but the first couple miles of Highway 64 were lined with strip joints, cannabis shops, adult entertainment salons, and massage parlors. It was seedy. I suppose those kinds of places weren't allowed in Fort Smith, and that is why they were concentrated over on the Oklahoma side of the Arkansas

River. At any rate, it was not a great "Howdy do." Well… unless one was looking for that sort of entertainment.

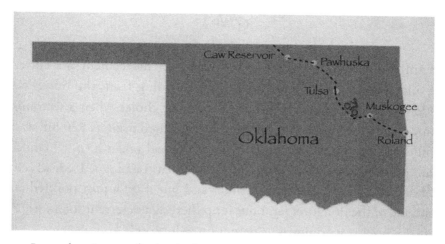

I was hoping to find a hideout soon as it was getting late, and I was weary from a long day of biking. I found a spot in Roland, but it was edgy. I had to push my bike through an area that looked like an abandoned homeless encampment. I kept going back into the woods in hopes of getting far enough that no one would care to pursue me. There was not a lot of bramble so the going wasn't too tough. I set up my tent in a nice clearing but with a mild feeling of trepidation. I had not seen anyone, so I stayed there. I had crossed some pretty damp ground and thought that no one else would be idiot enough to come back there.

75 miles.

I broke camp early and backtracked for a breakfast at McDonald's. They were not allowing inside seating, but I asked the manager if he could make an exception. After all, there was no place to sit outside, and I was on my bicycle. There was a little spot that kept me hidden from the counter area, and he allowed me to sit there. Yet another much-appreciated kindness.

I am all for making rules, but I think strict enforcement is a curse. I once had an employee who I caught stealing from the business. He was a good worker, but he made a poor choice when a seeming opportunity to make a little extra cash presented itself. A $20 bill was pilfered from our donation jar. I knew he had taken it, but I could not prove it. However, a long time before that, I had taped a dead cell phone to a dead mini-tape recorder and put it on a post pointed at the site of the donation jar. I put it up there as a deterrent for another thief who was working as a "detention volunteer."

I asked the suspect employee to help me take it down so that I could look at it. He thought he was caught red-handed. The next day, I asked him to stay a few minutes after work. He sat in the front office and simmered as I apologized and went upstairs to my office. I needed a few minutes because I had no idea what to say to him even though we both had had the whole night to think about it.

When I returned downstairs, I simply asked him if he had anything to tell me. In a panic he admitted to the theft. The poor guy had been stewing all the night before. I told him he needed to return the money, which he did right then. Then I asked him what he would do if he were me. He said, "I would fire me." I told him that he did good work and that I didn't want to do that. I stressed that we couldn't really tolerate any more of this, but that I wished to keep him on. After that, he was one of my best employees for years. One can only fight darkness by turning on a light.

I rode Truckee from Roland down to Highway 64. It was a very nice route. Like before, Interstate 40 took away most of the traffic. At Gore I crossed the Arkansas River once again headed for Tulsa. I would have been more inclined to find my way into Kansas by routing myself straight in-between Tulsa and Oklahoma City, but a friend of a good friend had invited me to have a break in Tulsa. I had met Pam once before in Alaska at our mutual friend's house. She had heard about my bicycle odyssey and offered a respite.

After Webber Falls, GMB beckoned me onto a freeway ramp. I rode part way up the ramp, but it did not feel right. GMB showed me getting onto Highway 351, but this looked more like an Interstate onramp. The Interstate ramps in the eastern US always have signs that say pedestrians, bicycles, and scooters are prohibited. This one had no such signage. It felt like permission. Another cause for doubt was a speed limit sign that said minimum speed 60. GMB showed it as a shortcut to Muskogee, and I took it.

I was exhilarated with a 16-MPH tailwind. These superhighways always have a very wide shoulder and a rumble strip on the traffic side of it. Even with the traffic going 70 miles per hour, it feels safe to me because I basically have a full lane all to myself. I rode at incredible speed for about 18 miles with no possibility to get off. I did not know that I was on the Muskogee Turnpike until I came to a tollbooth.

Oops!

There was no way to avoid the booth—no secret access road for tollbooth personnel. A nice lady came out of the little building and told me that it was against the law to ride a bicycle on the toll road and that she had to call the police. I had to wait for the police to arrive. The booth personnel were nice enough to top off my water bottles.

I might have been tempted to just ride down the side road and save everyone the trouble, but there was none.

I had to wait a long while. Part of our normal mental state is that we can sit and dream up many kinds of outcomes: arrest, court, jail, fines, 20 lashes. It is called worry, and it never helps—ever. It is mental calisthenics, but it is exercise that is damaging. People who engage in it usually pass their anxiety off onto others in some negative display of anguish—even harm. A friend might tell you that you have a right to worry. Well, you do, but that still makes both of you wrong. When we are young, we are taught punishment and reward, and that is what leads to this thwarting of equanimity. In truth, you do not know what is going to happen, and accepting that leads to peace of mind. Understand this and you can pass peace onto others instead of torment. Your life will immediately become better, and it will help those around you. It is not that hard. It is just unusual.

I learned this quite late in life, but I have enjoyed the lesson. Do I worry sometimes? Yes. But when I catch myself, I can see it for what it is and let go of it. It takes some practice, but it is achievable by everyone.

The state trooper rolled up in a regular sedan squad car. He got out and asked for my driver's license. We both could see that this bicycle with all my junk and me were not going to fit in the vehicle without a lot of effort. I told him that there were no signs indicating the prohibition of bicycles where I got on, and that I would never have gotten on if there were. Also, once I did get on, there were no more exits for me to get off. I told him that I had ridden there from Florida and that this situation was a first for me.

He stood there giving no indication of what he was thinking. I had pled my case. At this point he was the judge and jury.

He discharged this responsibility admirably. He told me that there was an off-ramp four miles further. He told me to get off there and stay off the turnpike. Justice was served, and I was not arrested. I was back on my way. I happily obliged and exited the turnpike as fast as I possibly could.

I got off at East Hancock Road. GMB led me through several miles of back roads and bike paths that bypassed Muskogee, so I never got to meet any Okies from there. The paths led me on to Highway 62, which eventually led me back onto my old friend Highway 64. I had a good tailwind that carried me to Haskell just before dark.

There were not any useful woods coming into Haskell. It seemed bereft of good stealth camping opportunities, though I did not give any much opportunity to emerge. It was a long day of riding, and I was too tired to go any further. I chose the entranceway to a church that was not far from the road. It was a longish, covered entrance. I was quite exposed there, but mostly to the backs of some buildings along the highway. I did not set up my tent. The prediction was for 66 degrees in the morning, so to stay more ensconced, I stacked my mats and sleeping bag on the cement behind a support column.

I had arrived at the church just before sundown, so it was not until later that I discovered I was camped under a motion detection light. The first time I rolled over in my sleeping bag the lights came on. This was way less than ideal for someone supposedly stealth camping, but I was way too bushed to relocate. I just stayed there with the light coming on every now and then. Thankfully, it did not draw anyone's attention.

85 miles.

CHAPTER 9

GoFundMe

Except for the motion detection light, it was still dark when I broke camp on Day 27. The motion lights provided good light for packing the bike. I rolled up to the Sunrise Café and barely had to wait for them to open. It was a pleasure to get a great veggie omelet and coffee so early. It was not going to be a long day. Tulsa was only about 35 miles away. Pam had informed me that it didn't matter when I arrived as she was working from home because of COVID.

I got back on good old Highway 64 and connected to the Riverwalk Trail in Tulsa. It was on this beautiful biking/walking trail that I crossed the Arkansas River for the seventh time. I traveled along the river on an excellent trail for miles. It was upriver, but the grade was negligible. Then there was a long arduous climb up to Pam's house.

38 miles.

Day 28 was a non-riding day. I had taken four days off riding back in Brandon, Mississippi, so I had ridden 23 out of 28 days, and I had covered 1,248 miles. That meant that I had ridden an average of 54 miles per riding day. Not bad for an old gimpy guy.

Pam was an excellent hostess. She took me on a driving tour around town to see the sights. I was even able to wash my sleeping bag after only 11 days of use. We had delicious Thai food, and I even got to sip some whiskey. And two nights out of the elements! I thought about staying a third night, but I was rested and ready to hit the road.

0 miles.

On Day 29, we went out for a nice, early breakfast replete with photo ops. It was not bad at all leaving on Wednesday morning. Once I got down near the river, it was straight and flat on bicycle trails all the way to Skiatook.

I stopped in the Walmart in Skiatook and picked up some insulin. Insulin will keep for 30 days if you don't let it freeze or get too hot. Under normal usage, a bottle would not last me nearly that long, but this constant exercise called for a lot less insulin. This was Day 29 and time to trade out. I did not know when I would hit another Walmart to resupply. I pay $25 for a bottle of 70/30 insulin at Walmart that would cost $100 at other pharmacies. I don't really know how this pricing works. It looks like collusion between insurance companies and pharmacies. God bless the US.

About 10 miles out of Skiatook on Highway 20, GMB suggested a series of back roads. I took the alternate paved road suggested by the app, but then it soon turned into a dirt road. In my mind the caution flags went up. Once again, it was good hard dirt road, but what if it got worse? After all, this was meant to be a bicycle adventure, not a study in abnegation.

It was rolling, hill-and-dale, cattle country. There were very few trees, and the area was flecked with oil-field pumps. Most of the hills were such that I could ride over them without having to dismount. I hardly saw anyone, but I did see a ranch house in the distance every now and then. I figured I could always go to one of those houses if I got in real trouble.

At the top of one rise near a gate, I decided to have a little nap on my mat. After a while, a fellow came along in his pickup truck. He was out checking his cattle and was bemused to see this bicycle guy lying there. It was a first for him. We had a nice chat. I told him I was headed for Denver. That was unbelievable enough, much less saying Seattle. He told me that the rest of the way on these roads was more or less in the condition I had already encountered. That was good to know—rideable. I thanked him for that information, and he went on his way.

I did not run into anyone else for the next 15 miles. It was easy enough going. The light wind was going to be against me regardless, so I wasn't in a hurry to find my way out to a paved road. I probably traveled for 20 miles on dirt roads before I got through that beautiful, sparse land and onto Highway 99. Wynona, Oklahoma was the next place to look for a stealth camp for the night.

There was a post office and the Wynona Stop Buy—a gas station/convenience store—and nothing else in the form of public services that I could tell. I rolled out to the First Baptist church but found it surrounded by houses. I even found a Kenneth Street on the edge of town, but nowhere along there to hide out. It was not a good spot, but I elected to stay between a large truck and an armory building. I wondered why there was an armory there. If a national enemy had made it to Wynona, Oklahoma, it might be time to surrender.

Perhaps it was difficult to mow between the building and the truck and some other junk that was around there, but the weeds and grass had gotten tall enough to give me something of a hideout. It was plenty good for sleeping.

48 miles.

I started out the day sipping bad coffee with good people. I wasn't in a hurry to get going because it was only 10 miles to Pawhuska, and I did not want to get there before the library opened. I had decided in the night that I was going to start a GoFundMe. The cost of a trip like this fell outside of my annual budget since in addition to trip costs I would have to get myself, my bike, and most of my stuff back to Florida. I save a lot of money by rarely paying for a motel room, but eating out a lot drives my expenses up.

Friends had told me that I should get a GoFundMe account for a trip like this right from the beginning. But what if I started an account and started raising funds and then wanted to quit because it was too damn difficult of a ride? I'm no youngster, and I was asking a lot of my old body. I did not want that hanging over my head. I would not have wanted to let people down. Now I had ridden over 1,300 miles, and I knew that, barring an unforeseen cataclysm, I was going to finish. I was not even close to halfway, and I had held Denver in my mind as a reasonable target for quitting. I had friends there to help me, and an airport. But I knew myself well enough to know that if I made it to Denver, I would just keep going.

The Wynona Stop Buy was busy, and the loaded bike and I attracted a lot of attention. I was still far from any XC bike route, so the sight was very unusual. I entertained lots of very friendly questions and conversations. This was one of the first places that someone asked me how old I was, and when I told him 69, he said, "Well, you're old enough to know better. Ha, ha." I would hear that several more times on this trip.

I got to the library in Pawhuska as it was opening, and they let me log onto a computer. I opened a GoFundMe account and named it "Route 69." In the opening, I asked for funds for getting me and my stuff back to Florida and a little bit more for some weather-dodging accommodation. I dedicated my trip to World Peace.

I had learned from my mentors that if you wanted to change the world, you had to change yourself first. There is no other way. You cannot promote peace until you can find it in yourself. I am far from perfect, but I have learned how to watch myself, and I give in to reactive behavior less and less. The idea that I might be able to impact World Peace helps power me. If you do not step outside of yourself, you can plan on living a "normal" life—a life aligned with strife instead of grace. Benevolence and angst are choices. Who would have thought? Which would you prefer?

I am not a social media kind of guy, so I just gave GoFundMe the names of everyone in my phone. The site would report my trip to my contacts, and then they could decide whether supporting an old man with post-polio and diabetes crossing the country on his bicycle was worthy of support.

I left Pawhuska's very nice library and went downtown. I had asked at the library if there was a good cup of coffee to be had down there. They recommended that I try The Mercantile.

It was Friday, and something must have been going on. Downtown was very busy with a lot of tourist-looking people. I stopped in at The Mercantile. It was a great place that was opened by the "Pioneer Woman," Ree Drummond. After hearing about her I wish I could have met her. She is an author and a blogger and sounds like a character.

The barista at The Mercantile was excited to hear that I was cycling cross-country and wanted to talk about it more. I told her that I would be sitting outside at one of their tables if she got a break. She never made it out, but I asked some people to take a picture of me and my bicycle in front of a restored, old-time pickup truck. I sat at a table outside with my Americano enjoying wonderful conversations.

A gentleman came up and asked me about the cycling, and I suggested he join me at my little table. I offered to buy him a coffee. He sat down, and we chatted for a long time. It turned out he was from Jacksonville, Florida, which is not far from where I started this journey. He asked me what I was doing in Pawhuska, and I told him that I had just gone to the library and started a GoFundMe. We were there until we both finished our coffees. When he got up, he handed me 20 bucks "toward my GoFundMe" and wished me well on my trip.

I rode up a hill leaving Pawhuska, and at the top the geography changed completely. I was going due west on Highway 60. The road was very straight, and the contour had turned into very long, shallow hills. There was not a shred of shade anywhere, and it was hot. I had not expected the relentlessness of it. My water was running out, and I presumed there was no place short of Ponca City to resupply. I came upon a couple of guys with trucks working in some capacity for the electric company. I asked them if they had any water to spare, and they were happy to load me up. I made a mental note to keep closer tabs on my water supply. Perhaps it was time to start filling my Camelback bladder. I had made it to the more expansive and parched western states. From here on there was an increased likelihood of running out of water.

I departed Highway 60 on Kaw Dam Road. I did not know of the dam and reservoir. It was amazing to bike across the dam. On the other side were the McFadden Cove Campgrounds, where I would spend the night. It was here that I was reminded why I preferred my stealth camps in the woods to official campgrounds. The campgrounds with people in their campers with electric hookups tend to be noisier into the night. After they quieted, the coyotes took to howling. That noise is preferable and even soothing. I noticed before I hit the sack that my GoFundMe was already over half funded!

48 miles.

As usual, I left early in the morning. I was headed out on Lake Road hoping someone might have the coffee pot on. I was happy to quickly come across the Lakeview Campground Store and Bait Shop. It was owned and staffed by a very congenial couple who were curious about my bike adventure. I purchased some items, and they gave me free coffee. I even learned a few things. Kaw Lake was named after the Kaw Indian Tribe. The tribe is closely related to the Osage Nation, which were the principles in Pawhuska. Pawhuska was the name of an Osage chief, and the name Kansas was derived from Kaw. I also learned about a huge fish in the reservoir that I had never heard of.

I saw pictures around the shop of a giant fish they called a spoonbill. It is officially called the American paddlefish and is closely related to the sturgeon. I would have considered myself a knowledgeable fishing person, but I had never heard of it. They average over four feet long and 60 pounds. The record was set in June of 2021 at 164 pounds in the Keystone Reservoir a little further south in Oklahoma.

Fresh with new knowledge that I would not have obtained had I not been on this bike trip, I headed north toward Kansas.

I took a series of good, paved roads that seemed made for XC cycling. They kept me off the busier Highway 77 for a while. Eventually, I cut over to Highway 77 because I knew it would have a "Welcome to Kansas" sign when I got that far. It is one thing to whiz by a state's welcoming sign in your car, but it feels like a necessary photo-documentation for biking.

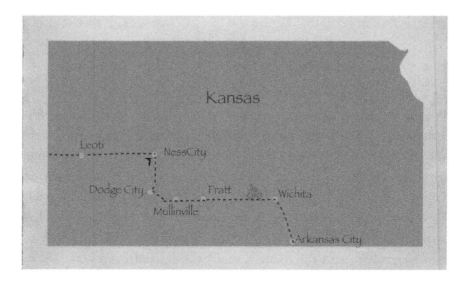

I entered Arkansas City, Kansas on Highway 77. There I crossed the Arkansas River again. But it turns out that in Kansas they call it the ar-Kansas River, emphasis on the Kansas part. Then GMB took me through town on some lesser roads that did not provide the sustenance I now needed. I steered toward Kate's Café but found it closed. GMB put me on Highway 166, and I continued until I came to the Green-Door La Familia Mexican Restaurant. It was very busy—right at lunch time. I was starving by now and hungrily pushed my way in. Thank goodness it turned out to be a terrific stop. The food was excellent, and the service was terrific. I ordered fajitas, and they brought me a tremendous amount of food, which was exactly what I needed. I thought maybe I had ordered for two, but it didn't matter. On a trip like this, it would have been difficult for a place to bring me a serving I couldn't finish.

Sated, I left Arkansas City on a combination of small roads that eventually took me to Highway 3 where I came to a pivotal intersection. It felt ominous. There was absolutely nothing there. Just an intersection in the countryside with nothing in any direction and a choice. If I continued north on 3, it would take me into Wichita. If I went west on 142nd Road, I would end up in Dodge City.

I had a somewhat romantic interest in going to Dodge City. A favorite western television series of my youth, *Gunsmoke,* was set there. From other movies, Dodge City was reminiscent of the old, Wild West. Stopping at this intersection in the middle of nowhere, there was a decision to make. I kind of wanted to pass through Dodge City even though it would only satisfy a figment of my imagination. I laughed at the absolute meaninglessness of my conundrum and just continued north. Pragmatism won. I had a 15-MPH tailwind if I kept going north. A series of decisions along my new chosen route would make my indecision at this intersection more laughable.

I sipped an iced coffee from a can in Udall and then got on Highway 15 to head northwest toward Mulvane. As I was crossing a railroad bridge on Rock Road, a huge freight train was starting to pass under. I was there in plenty of time to take a video of it on my phone. I have a fondness for trains, and this was a thrill. Others crossing over it in automobiles would hardly notice. I love the feel of all that power and momentum cascading just below me.

Nighttime was getting close, and I needed to look for a hideout. Not far outside of town at E95th Street, there came a good, wooded corner. I turned and looked for an easy way into the woods. I chose a spot where I thought I could push through the brush, and I waited until there were no cars around and I pushed. I went 200 feet back to a great spot. Someone might spot me in the morning pushing back out, but I didn't care. It was a beautiful stealth camp.

I had to smile at the quandary I had had today at that intersection. Dodge City/Wichita? We all make decisions like that regularly, mostly without noticing. We are all at some crossroads in our lives all the time, but we rarely think of it in those terms. On the way to Port Townsend, Washington, does it matter if I pass through Dodge City or Wichita? Essentially, it doesn't.

Or does it? I made today's decision based on the wind direction—a common criterion for XC bicycle travel choices. Everything henceforth is a consequence of that choice. It is fun to think about. It can make a dramatic difference.

In an earlier, foreign travel adventure, my travel partner Debbie and I found ourselves on the coast of the Malaysian Peninsula at Mersing. It sounded like it would be fun to take the ferry out to Tioman Island for a while to get away from roads and crowds. What is not to love about a tropical island in good weather?

We went out for a week. The ocean and sky were beautiful, and the bungalows were sufficient. I spent most of my time snorkeling around the stunning coral heads not far off the beach. Indonesia and Malaysia had the best snorkeling I had ever experienced.

One day, I spotted an anchor on the bottom that a fishing boat had probably lost. It was in about 30 feet of water, and it looked like a 50-pounder. Things are easier to lift underwater, so I dove down and picked it up and walked backwards toward shore—backwards because I had fins on. I repeated this many times until I had the anchor on the beach.

Sure enough, someone came along and wanted it. My command of the language of Malaysia was woefully rudimentary, so after many smiles and friendly hand gestures, I let him take it. I should have started a business because over the course of my stay, I brought two more anchors to shore.

We were still out at Tioman when the tropical fantasy collided with the monsoon. Like flipping a switch, the weather went from perfect to horrible. After two days of wind and rain and dark gray, we decided to leave the island, as did everyone else.

It was a long time ago, and the ferry was a very heavy, wooden boat about 60 feet long. In this terrible weather, the captain had to bring it alongside a dock that looked more like an old, tired assemblage of pencils.

I had a lot of experience in Alaska boating in shitty weather, and I admired the captain's skill. He came up to the leeward side of the dock so the wind would not push him through it. Each time he came up to the dock, three or four people would hop aboard before the wind pushed him away, and he had to reapproach the collection of sticks.

When everyone who wanted to leave Tioman Island was on board, or at least those who were up for a perilous, nauseating boat ride, we left. Once we were away from the island, we could see nothing but slate gray in every direction. Gray ocean and gray clouds dumping voluminous gray rain. We had a following sea that made waves like herds of huge elephants traveling under the boat from behind. The cabin was packed full of people, but that was not why we didn't go inside. I had heard plenty of stories from all over the world where passenger ferries capsized and all but a few drowned. Instead, we sat on a bench that went across the very back of the boat—with masks and snorkels in hand. I noted that if we did end up in the water, the way to shore was to go with the wind. With masks and snorkels, there was a chance for survival. If the boat capsized, people in the cabin had virtually no chance.

The ferry was an astonishing example of solid boat-building. It was likely to survive just about any catastrophe in one piece. Not so much the passengers. However, anyone sitting outside was getting drenched in rain and spray. Thankfully, the water from both the sea spray and sky was warm.

Debbie took a break from extreme nausea to exclaim, "A man just fell overboard!" A Malaysian guy had been sitting on the gunnel just outside the cabin entrance. Maybe he had been sitting there because no one else would fit in the cabin. At any rate, I watched him drift past as the captain tried the impossible task of stopping the boat in the heavy, following sea. The man was swimming after the boat in a panic with absolutely no chance of catching us. I scrambled around the back of the boat looking for anything floatable that I could throw to the man who was now getting further and further behind us.

There was nothing! Not one thing! I had noticed a bundle of jerry jugs on the bow when I had boarded, but it was already too late to cut them loose. In this wind they would have just skidded atop the ocean ahead of the boat.

The man disappeared in the gray.

The captain started to turn the boat around to go back for the guy, and this was the first time I felt real peril. For the boat to turn around, it would have to get into the trough twice. It would have to go sideways between these huge waves two times! A lesser boat would likely roll over. If we survived turning around, we still had to find the guy. It seemed impossible.

Nevertheless, after what felt like forever, they spotted him, and the captain started his approach. The crew went to the front of the boat in hopes of plucking the guy out. I found a long tie-up line in a box in the back of the boat. I wedged myself at the back corner of the cabin and coiled the line for throwing. It didn't seem necessary, but I did it anyway.

The boat was about 45 feet abreast of the guy when a terrific herd of elephants ran underneath the vessel and carried us too far forward for the crew to get him. Now he was about 45 feet from me, and the next wave was going to take us far beyond his rescue. He was no longer even trying to swim to the boat. I believe he was completely spent.

When I reflect on the incident, I think about all the line-throwing practice I had in Alaska. We even threw lines at beer cans on the dock for fun. We considered it great sport.

I threw the tie-up line right across his shoulder. He only had to reach up and grab it. It seemed to be all he had strength for. As I started to pull him to the boat, the crew showed up and helped me. We all grabbed the gunnel and a fistful of his clothing and hoisted him onto the deck. He was exhausted, but he was alive!

The boat returned to its heading for Mersing, and I returned to my vigil on the bench at the stern of the boat—mask and snorkel in hand. We still had a long way to go, and we had to cross a sandbar with these huge waves pushing us.

I was back to feeling reasonably safe. Even if we went to shit crossing the sandbar, I felt like I had what it took to get myself and my travel partner from the sandbar to the shore.

The man who had fallen overboard lay on the deck between the gunnel and the cabin and did not move even as we crossed the sandbar and the boat hit bottom. The next wave picked us up and thunked us on the bottom again. I could see him breathing. He was still alive, and I wondered what he thought of all of this. The next wave picked us up and carried us safely on.

At the dock everyone got busy with disembarkation, including us. We wanted to make our way out of the monsoon, which meant getting across the Malaysian Peninsula. We had a long way to go in flooding conditions. I left before the man got up, and no one spoke to me.

So, our decision to go to Malaysia and to Tioman Island, and even to board the boat in that horrible weather, led to my intersection with that man's life. My training in Alaska, my lack of fear of the water, and a zillion experiences of things going wrong put me at the corner of that cabin with the coiled rope in hand. I don't know that I saved that man's life, but I doubt he could have survived us going around and trying to find him again. The circumstances had not favored it.

We really cannot parse out our experiences in any meaningful way. They are beautifully mysterious. As I stood at that bare road intersection having to choose between Dodge City and Wichita, I had to smile at the choice. The differences it makes in circumstances are blessedly ineffable.

71 miles.

Just after getting off Highway 15 in Wichita, I crossed the Arkansas River again. GMB put me on some terrific bike paths, and I made my way through Wichita with amazing ease. The paths followed the river through the city, and I crossed it two more times. The total number of crossings was now 10. It was the weekend, and lots of people were taking advantage of the many lovely spots along the river. There were lots of ducks and geese. I'm not sure everyone would be so happy with the waterfowl. They can make quite a minefield out of a recreation area.

I left town on Zoo Blvd to W. 21st Street. These were long, straight roads that sped me out of town. At one point I stopped at a Starbucks, and while I was sitting at a table outside with my coffee, I notice that the barista had written "Happy Biking" on the cup. A small, welcome delight!

West 21st Street took me a long way out of town, and when it snaked beneath a huge dike for the Cheney Reservoir, it turned into Northeast 50th Street. Before long, I came to the West Side Bait Shop & Beer. I had a nice meal there and asked if there were showers available in the Cheney State Park. They told me there were, so I went in. Getting a shower on my fourth day without was going to be great.

It was an expansive park with many camping areas. I checked the shower facilities at each one, but all were locked. I couldn't find anyone to ask until I stumbled upon the campground hosts. Seeing my predicament, Diane hopped in her car and drove to other parts of the giant lakeside park. She came back and said that none of them were working and that I could just share their spot. So, I got my shower and spent an awesome time with them. They were excited to hear bicycle trip stories, and it was fun to hear how she had gotten disillusioned with the East Coast of the US and ended up coming to Kansas and lucking into her husband Lyle. My time with them was pure joy. Also, it rained in the night, and I got to miss it.

49 miles.

I didn't leave at first light this time because I wanted to say a proper goodbye at a reasonable hour to my marvelous hosts Diane and Lyle. They were a highlight of my trip. We said our goodbyes, and I was again on my way.

I had come into Kansas on the southeast end. I intended to go out midway on the western side. I kept GMB focused on Eads, Colorado. I figured I would randomly take different roads north and west to get across Kansas on a diagonal zigzag. However, in the morning when I started out, the wind was 15 MPH out of the north, and there was no sense fighting it if I didn't have to. I would keep going west on little NW 50th Street. It was a perfect two-lane road with no shoulder and no traffic. But also, there were no services.

When I was getting hungry, I took North Berry Avenue down to Kingman, Kansas. It was a town large enough to have good services, and I stopped at Jeri's Kitchen for a meal. I left my bicycle parked out by the entrance and locked it. I carry a little cable lock that would only keep the honest people honest. I wasn't worried about locking it to anything because the whole ensemble weighed nearly 100 pounds. And really, even if I did not lock it, it would be the rare thief that would have been able to ride off on it. Heck, it was difficult enough for me to ride off on it. Getting started was not easy.

A woman at the next table struck up a conversation with me. She made the association of a loaded bike outside and a guy inside with stretch shorts and a blinding bright bike shirt. I think that riding in anything other than bright yellow, bright orange, and/or bright green is nuts.

Of course, the first questions were where from and where to. Florida/Denver. She was floored. The next question was the more difficult one to answer. "Why?" Yes, why would anyone ride a bicycle across the country? Since I couldn't come up with a good reason, I just said, "Why not?!" I'm sure she could have come up with a list of reasons why not as long as her arm. But I could see right away that she got it. We and her companions had a fun conversation. When I got up to leave, she insisted on buying my lunch.

At these encounters some people could not resist asking me my age, though these folks did not. I don't blame people for being curious…I would be. And after this conversation, "Why not?" became my stock answer to the question "Why," which I was asked often. Sometimes, for fun, I would say, "Well, I'm just riding my bike over to my friend's house."

I left Kingman on Highway 400, which was a major thoroughfare. It had a good shoulder, and it was not terrible for traffic. Besides, I still could not go north because the wind had come up to north 22. For me, riding against a 20-MPH wind is like riding a stationary bike. A 20-plus MPH wind straight on my side is tolerable. It is just that it wants to blow me into the road or into the ditch depending on which side.

Radar showed a big storm approaching from the west, so I raced to Pratt and took a motel room. I guess I was looking for comfort in my old age. I was more relaxed about it because my GoFundMe was already fully funded, and weather-dodging accommodation was one of the reasons I started it.

56 miles.

I stayed at the Comfort Suites and had their continental breakfast before I rolled out to find a good coffee. I did not drink coffee until I was in my 40s, but prior to that, I had served my caffeine addiction with sweet colas. It probably supported my becoming diabetic. I have replaced sugary sodas with coffee and cream.

Pratt was large enough to have a medical facility. Usually if a place is large enough to have one, there is likely to be one or more coffee shops of top quality. At the shop I found I was telling my travel story to a patron, and the owner overheard and was impressed. She deemed one of her scones to not be of sellable quality, and she gave it to me. Who doesn't love a second-rate scone?! I super-enjoyed it later down the road.

I often wonder what this bike trip would be like without coffee. I go out of my way a lot, and it is somewhat expensive. A line in my GoFundMe ask should have been, "and to support my coffee addiction." There is no doubt that at times I can be dragging along on Truckee and then input some coffee and tear off down the road. Of course, I rationalize my addiction, telling myself it is not impinging on anyone else.

I recognize, though, that I have an addictive personality. I have spent an amazing amount of time working crossword puzzles and sudoku puzzles. I wondered what I did with all that time before I took up the puzzles. Computers did not come into my life before I was an adult, so when they did, I was disciplined enough to just erase the games off them, or to not open the games in the first place.

I was also addicted to pinball in my youth. But with pinball you always had to put a quarter in the machine to play, and there was not an endless stockpile of quarters. I had to earn, borrow, or steal my supply just like with any addiction.

Nowadays, there is no clear up-front cost of video games to a child. No quarters necessary. The parents contribute $70 per month plus devices, and the child can play video games until they go blind, or their fingers fall off. The deleterious effects are clear, but the devices make great babysitters. However, it is rare to see a child give up their device without a fit or an earnest round of bargaining. The reaction to any addiction. That is how I would have been. I am interested to see how this plays out over the long run.

I had to keep going west on Highway 400 because there was still a strong wind from the north. It had a little bit of easterly to it, so I was getting a teeny push. The irony was not lost on me that days before, I had cause to choose between Wichita and Dodge City and that I chose Wichita. Now, because of these fierce northerly winds, I was almost certainly going to end up in Dodge City after all. So much for that decision point days ago at the "ominous intersection."

Hours later, I was in Mullinville. I went into town in search of water. The wind had slackened somewhat, so I thought it might be interesting to take some back roads again. I'm glad I chose to leave the main highway there because I was startled to come upon the art of M. T. Liggett. It was an enormous collection of sculptures made from found metals welded together in whatever fashion had struck him. Many of them were jointed to move with the wind. It could not fail to impress, especially coming upon it so unexpectedly. There must have been acres of them.

The only person I saw was at the shed where Liggett must have created the collection. He had since passed on. I asked the lady if I could get any water there and struck up a conversation. She had a refined elegance that I also would not have expected to find in this tiny country town. It turned out that she was working for a museum in New Orleans where she lived. She was a curator—there to manage Liggett's art for a collection. I felt a little bad for her because she was not in her element in Mullinville, and it showed. She had been stuck there for quite a while.

I got water from a hose, but the quality was extremely poor. I would hang on to it and only use it if I had to. Bad water is a lot better than none. I would dump it out later when I could get better water.

I zigzagged over some decent back roads and came back out to Highway 400 just below Ford, Kansas. There was a decent-looking restaurant there, and I arrived just in time to see the closed sign placed in the window. I was relegated to some unfortunate selections at the convenience store next door. The guy behind the counter was very affable when I asked him about possible camping in the area. He said he couldn't give me permission, but people sometimes camped adjacent to the restaurant parking lot.

Good enough. I set my tent up back there and enjoyed a beautiful, quiet sunset.

59 miles.

Day 35.

Last night, not long after I had slipped into my sleeping bag, a semitruck pulled into the parking lot. He spent the night there too, but he left his noisy engine running all night! Needless to say, my rest was uneven, but it made it easier for me to get up at 5:15 and break camp. The convenience store opened, and I was able to perform my ablutions. I had a nice chat with the clerk, and she gave me my coffee for free, lovely! Next stop—Dodge City.

In an amazing stroke of luck, the wind was coming out of the south… just when I needed it! God bless a tailwind! It was a little chilly, but once I got going, I took my gloves off and managed to drop one without knowing it. Before long, a car pulled off ahead of me, and the driver, a young lady, stepped out. She handed me the glove that I didn't even know I had lost. She had seen me drop it. I could tell she was in a bit of a hurry, but I asked her where she was from. She said Mullinville. I asked her if she knew M. T. Liggett. She gave me an odd, disappointed look and left without answering. She had certainly done me a welcomed favor. I had run into so many nice people in Kansas that I thought the state should be called Kindness.

I had ridden past about a zillion acres of wheat, but this area was a little drier. It was more cattle country. Within a mile or two, I was surprised to find myself crossing the Arkansas River again. Remember though—it is called the "ar-Kansas" river here. I think this was my 11th crossing and most likely my last. It was a barely damp creek at this point with a beautiful sunrise behind it. Shortly after crossing the creek, I ran into my first tumbleweed of the trip. It was an omen. I was getting close to the other symbol of the Wild West—Dodge City.

I passed through a lot of cattle country, and though I had not had one in a decade, I found myself craving steak. I presume the constant workout had something to do with it. I thought that I ought to be able to get a real good one in Kansas—one that had not suffered taste degradation from having been frozen.

One of the many jobs I had in my life was as an assistant manager at a McDonald's restaurant when I was 19 years old. The store I worked at in Sarasota, Florida had just swapped from fresh hamburger to cryogenically frozen hamburger. Yes, serving fresh hamburger was logistically difficult. This was 50 years ago. They said that flash freezing locked in flavor better.

Months later, I was down in Miami, and I stopped at a McDonald's there and purchased a quarter pounder. In one bite I could not believe how much better the Miami burger was than ours up north. It was the old Golden Arches style building where you could see in the kitchen.

I looked in the back and saw them laying fresh patties on the grill. They had not gone to the cryogenically frozen meat yet. At least in terms of flavor, cryogenics was a bill of goods.

As I came into Dodge City from the south, I rode between a giant feed lot and an even bigger processing plant. Before I got into town, I rode past another gigantic meat-packing plant. Both places had an ocean of freezer vans parked outside. There was also a huge rail yard that served both. The numbers are staggering. I read that those two plants process 10,000 head of cattle per day! Six days a week! A vegetarian's nightmare.

I made it to Dodge City by 8:30 in the morning and was surprised and a little disappointed that I had to wait until 9 a.m. for Miss Kitty's Diner to open. Clearly not a workingman's breakfast spot. It was more of a tourist stop. When I finally got inside, I found it completely decorated in *Gunsmoke* paraphernalia. Pictures of Matt Dillon, Miss Kitty, Doc Adams, and all were ubiquitous.

The crew was very friendly and helped me get my devices plugged in. My server could not have been 20 years old. She was very modern-looking—bleach blonde Hispanic with lots of makeup. No Old-West look for this young lady. (Well…I guess Miss Kitty always wore tons of makeup.) I wondered if my lovely young waitress had ever seen an episode of that iconic Western. I looked at steak and eggs on the menu and asked her if the steak was local. She gave me a perplexed look and a shrug. My dream of a never-frozen, local steak was shattered. I let it go and ordered the veggie omelet.

A person's happiness is governed wholly and solely by their ability to let go. Let go of what? Fear and desire. It is easy to see if you reverse engineer any desire. Let's say you really want a red BMW. It is on your mind all the time, and you work hard to save for it. When you finally get it, you are happy, but you think it is getting the car that made you that way when it is the ending of the desire that gave you the release. It is possible to bypass the desired object and go straight to the happiness. As an adult human that is entirely up to you.

I started this trip carrying a small, colorful drawstring pouch. It had bicycles printed on it and came with something I had purchased before the trip. I was carrying it just so I could give it away. Back in Alabama a woman pulled up at a gas station with two children strapped in car seats in the back. The little girl, about five years old, unbuckled herself and quite charmingly engaged me in conversation. She was captivated by my bicycle with all the luggage on it. Not considering her baby brother in the other car seat, I asked the woman if I could give the daughter the little pouch. She said yes, and I handed the lady the pouch. When she passed it back to the daughter, the little boy exploded in a fit of rage.

I could see that I had started something by my mistake of not having two pouches in that situation. Baby Caligula was too young to have any control over his behavior, but I have seen adults behave similarly without that excuse. As I was leaving, the little girl handed the screaming baby the pouch, which shut him up. The young girl let go of her attachment to the pouch for him, and he let go of his fury by getting it. We all carry subtle versions of those behaviors into adulthood. It is the letting go that quells them.

But are desires natural or OK? Of course. In the most existential sense, everything that is is. It doesn't really matter if you think it is OK or not. But I am addressing personal happiness here and a person's own ability to affect it. I will go one step further and add a truth that is difficult to demonstrate or prove. There is the potential to harbor desire with no possibility of dissatisfaction. It is desire that does no harm. If you have no attachment to the outcome, it will not affect you. You are in complete control if you let yourself be.

Chapter 10

Dorothy and Toto

The breakfast at Miss Kitty's hit the spot, and I was hitting the road. I was ecstatic to have a stiff, 13-MPH southerly wind. I would be able to make up for all the times I couldn't go north. I got on Highway 283 going straight north and left Dodge City in the dust. I stopped for lunch in Jetmore, and someone paid for my meal without identifying themselves. It felt weird to not have someone to thank, but I was grateful. Thank you!

In Ness City I would be turning west onto Highway 96 and would be joining the Adventure Cycling Associations TransAmerica Bike Route for about 150 miles.

10 miles before town, though, I saw some menacing, dark storms coming toward me from the northwest. They were black, apocalyptic-looking cells marching across the plain. There was absolutely nowhere to hide. The ditch was very shallow and the fields perfectly flat and wide open. There wasn't even a tree to cling to. I looked at the radar image on my phone and saw a line of angry red dots on the screen. They were bearing down on the little blue one—me. Was I going to join Dorothy and Toto?

I rode like hell. There was nothing else to do. If I went back, there was no guarantee that the storms would miss me, and there was no place to hide back behind me anyway. This was vacant land. I rode as fast as I could, keeping an eye out for any depression in the ground or something that was going to save my ass. I looked for a culvert that I could squeeze into where I would have to leave Truckee to fend for itself. I wasn't worried about getting wet in a ditch. These dots on the radar looked like tornados. I could feel and smell the weather changing.

I'll never say I am not lucky. I just kept pounding the pedals because there was nothing else to do. About a mile outside of town, I came upon the mostly dry Walnut Creek. It was a good depression, and there was a viaduct under the highway. I rushed Truckee down the hill and over to the opening. I spread my rain poncho on the ground and laid the bike on it. Then I dragged the bike a little way into the tunnel. I felt confident that I would be fine under there even if a tornado rolled right over me. I went up to the highway, sat, and waited.

I could not see a funnel cloud—just blackness approaching. You can watch videos of tornados all day, but you don't get to feel that sudden drop in barometric presure. I planned to drag my bike under the tunnel more vigorously if I did see one. The drama was exhilarating. I looked at the radar again, and now it appeared that I had ridden just far enough that the storm might barely miss me to the south. I started getting pelted with giant raindrops. Any minute I expected to see cows swirling past. The blackness was close enough to taste, but it moved on, leaving me energized and jubilant.

I rolled into Ness City to look for a place to spend the night. I checked out the Nazarene Church and the First Baptist Church. They were not going to work. I looped back to the United Methodist Church, and there were two men standing in the street. I asked them if they could suggest someplace to put up a tiny tent. One of them said there was a place on the right as you were leaving town on 96. "Cyclists sometimes set up in there."

Oh yeah. I was now on the TransAmerica cycling route, so most of these towns had regular XC cyclist visits. Along this road, I would not be such an odd sight. There are many cyclists each year going through here in one direction or the other on Highway 96.

I stopped at a convenience store and bought a sandwich and a beer and went to the end of town. The park was another steeper and deeper section of Walnut Creek. There were a couple picnic tables down in the bottom, but it would be too hard for me to get down there with my loaded bike and harder to get back out. I inspected an interesting structure at street level. It was like an unmaintained and somewhat dilapidated picnic shelter. I had difficulty getting the door open, but most of the screens were still up. It had a cement floor. Perfect!

I could not see the baseball park nearby, but I could hear cracks of a bat and cheering. It had a good feeling. People having fun.

While I was dining, some young guys came out of the woods and passed by my little homeless hotel. I had the distinct feeling that this was their target to hang out. I said hello to them, and they said hey back but kept going.

It was an excellent night. A bit chilly and very starry. My tornado tribulation was behind me. I wondered if there had been a funnel cloud hidden in all that blackness. I had not seen any cattle floating past. I slept very well.

71 miles.

The evening before, while I was looking around town for a place to stay the night, I had passed by a couple of cafés. I backtracked into town to find breakfast. It was very early, and the first one I came to, More Than Coffee, was not open yet. Thankfully, the Cuppa Joe was. I had a nice big meal there and plenty of coffee and then got back on 96 headed west.

Lots of people say that Kansas is flat, and if you are crossing it at 70 miles an hour in a vehicle, it would seem like it. But to those people, I would say, "Bike across it." It is really an endless series of long, gentle grades. It is not flat. The Mississippi Delta was flat. Level flat. But on

Truckee with 30 speeds and these gentle grades, I could always find the "sweet" gear for the circumstance. This was Day 36, and the ride had not lost its allure. Maintaining a comfortable speed while shifting up or down a gear or two is gratifying riding.

It was truly a lucky decision to leave my house on April 1. I was crossing Kansas in a variety of winds, but it was not hot. In another month or so, riding in the afternoons would be unbearably hot. I was riding in afternoon temperatures in the 60s, which was ideal.

Highway 96 was mostly straight with a railroad track following along it. I rode through Beeler and stopped in Dighton for a quick snack. I was ravenous when I got to Scott City in the late afternoon, and I was craving steak again. I don't usually crave foods, and never beef, so I thought my body must be telling me something. I turned into the downtown and right away saw Tate's Steakhouse. There was no deciding. I just parked Truckee out front and went in. It was very dark inside, and having come in from bright sun, I couldn't see anything. I tripped over the doorjamb and caught myself. Whoever might have been in there would have seen this, and I just looked up and laughed. I raised up my hands and said, "I'm alright," to my invisible audience. I felt my way to a table and sat down. The waitress was very friendly and took my steak and baked potato order. I knew I was losing weight, but I had no idea how much. It didn't really matter. I was quite overweight when I left my house.

The waitress brought me my meal, and I devoured it in the quiet dimness. Now I could see there were a few other people further into the restaurant. The meal was very good, and when I asked for the check, she said, "It's taken care of."

Huh? Again?! I asked her if there was someone I could thank. She paused. I think she wasn't supposed to say. A gentleman was just then passing by us headed out the door. She thumbed at him. I called out, "Thank you," and he was gone. I asked her if he had covered a tip as well. She was taking my plates away, and she smiled brightly and said, "Oh yes." I put down $5 anyway and left.

I rode another 16 miles or so west on 96. It was, again, wide-open country so there were no good hideouts. Somewhere past the turnoff for Modoc, I found a dirt road and turned north on it until I crossed the train tracks. There was nothing around there except fields. In the distance there was a huge wind farm. I was reasonably certain that if anyone saw me camping there, they wouldn't care. I leaned on my cane and kicked a flat spot in the corn stubble to make camp. It was a clear night with a chilly wind. The sun was setting on a cloudless horizon. The windmills slowly turned in unison, and as darkness fell, red lights shone at the top of each one. The lights were very bright. The enchantment of the giants dancing in place below the stars was transforming. The ingenious gentleman Don Quixote would be overwhelmed. But it was too cold in my little La Mancha to sit up any longer. Rocinante (Truckee) would have to keep vigil outside of my tiny tent.

71 miles.

My 20-year-old down bag wasn't enough on nights like this one. There were spots where the feathers had separated permanently, so I had to wear my jacket and long pants to bed some nights.

I was usually in bed at sundown, so I usually got up before sunrise. I rode the 11 miles to Leoti with a crisp southeast wind behind me. I passed the Wichita County Municipal Golf Course and gratefully came to the Route 96 Café. There was a big, round table inside with seven or eight "regulars" there. It was a collection of good ol' guys and gals from the area together enjoying the start to their day. There were a few other customers. I was very happy to get some coffee and start warming up. I ordered the usual omelet.

After a while, one of the fellas at the big table dragged me into their conversation. I went willingly. They, of course, wanted to know where I was from and where was I going. They were not strangers to cross-country cyclists. One of them asked me how old I was, and when I told them, one said, "Why, you're old enough to know better." They all laughed.

There was only one server in the place, and she really scrambled to keep up. Her service was great. Of course, she knew all the regulars. They all left while I finished my breakfast.

When it came time to go, the waitress said, "It's been taken care of." It was becoming a trend! I asked her if the tip was taken care of, and she said yes. I left her another $5 bill.

Just after Selkirk, Kansas, I crossed my second dateline into Mountain Time. It felt funny to stop the bicycle there. It is not lost on me that these datelines, state borders, and even country borders are just agreed-upon figments of our collective imaginations. In reality, there are no lines—dotted or otherwise. Can I really put one foot in 10 in the morning and the other in 11?

I traveled to Tribune, Kansas with the wind staying on my hindquarters. There had been a slight gain in elevation over the course of crossing Kansas. Wichita was 1,300 feet above sea level, and now Tribune was 3,543. Not a lot of elevation gain when it is spread out over all those miles. More noticeable was that the further west I got, the more desiccated became the terrain. Back in the eastern part of the state, the wheat was thick and green, and there were a lot more farms. Now, over similar long-distance views, there were fewer farmhouses, and any wheat fields looked stunted. Dry prairie was taking over.

I thought about the privilege of watching these changes by bicycle. People crossing Kansas by car would probably stop twice and have short, perfunctory conversations with a few counter people. I had just spent six days crossing the state, and while watching the landscape change, I had the warmest human interactions imaginable.

16 miles past Tribune, I crossed another imaginary line…

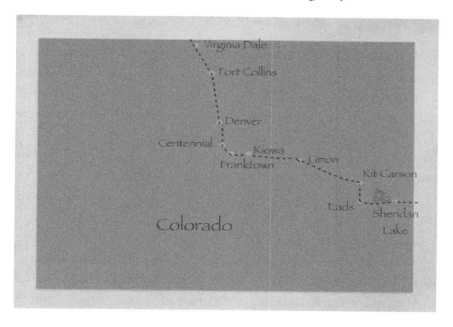

A friend of mine from Alaska was on a cross-country motorcycle trip traveling from Seattle through the southern United States and then up to New York. We had texted about meeting somewhere and were keeping track of each other via messaging. He was getting closer, and I had told him that I planned to turn north at Eads, Colorado.

Toby was no stranger to adventure. He had left the East Coast as a teenager and found his way to Alaska. He had worked in many capacities in Alaska's fishing industry, including king crab fishing on *Deadliest Catch*-style boats. We were both in the salmon fishing industry when we met at the cannery long ago. Since then, we had stepped in each other's footprints in nonprofits in the town of Kodiak. The last one was the Kodiak Maritime Museum Board.

It was getting toward dark, and I was looking for both water and a place to stay. The land had really dried out, and it looked like there was a lot of terrain that would be unusable without irrigation. Inclement weather was in the offing, including a possibility of snow in a few days. Spring storms in this area are legendary.

I biked past the town of Towner, which was just a collection of houses. This area was the site of the "Pleasant Hill Bus Tragedy" in 1931. It occurred on what started as a nice day, but a blizzard moved in. A school bus with 20 kids and the driver got lost in a blinding snowstorm and went into a ditch. They were stuck in the bus for 33 hours during the blizzard, and five children died of exposure. The bus driver left the bus to try to find help and died of exposure out in the elements. The spring weather in this part of the country is nothing to be trifled with.

In the town of Sheridan Lake, I arrived at the gas station after it had closed. There was nowhere to get water outside. The next place that had any services was Eads 28 miles ahead. I couldn't risk it. The wind had come up against me, and I knew that there wasn't a chance of making it without refilling my water bottles. The gas pumps were working, and a local fellow was there gassing up his pickup truck. I asked him if he knew of anywhere that I could get water. He said that there was a church in town that has water and puts up cyclists.

What luck! If I had the ACA route map, this church would have been on there as an excellent resource. I had just discovered it by accident.

I pedaled over to the Sheridan Lake Federated Church. It was unlocked, and there was a sign on the door welcoming cyclists. It was too good to be true. I walked in and was standing there in disbelief when the pastor came in to welcome me. He lived next door and had seen me ride up. He showed me around and said I could sleep on the floor wherever I wanted. He also said there were storms coming, and I could stay as long as needed. The place was spacious and spotless, and I felt like a grunge-bomb. My last shower was four days and 240 miles ago back in Pratt, Kansas.

After Pastor Ernie left, I spread my mats out along a wall next to an outlet. My solar-charging battery, though perched atop my handlebar extension, never really performed as I had hoped. It could ride there all day exposed to blinding sun and barely keep up with demand. Every four or five days, I had to plug it in somewhere. Sometimes I could charge my phone directly from it. Other times, I had to use it to charge my other battery and then charge my phone from that. These devices are mysterious to me not least because, for me, they rarely seem to work as advertised.

I had an excellent night indoors.

69 miles.

The NW 21-MPH wind showed up as promised on Saturday, Day 38. It was sunny and warm, but a cold front was predicted. I got up early and did all my garment handwashing. The church did not have showers, and I couldn't stand myself any longer. There was an alcove out one of the back doors which faced onto a few grain silos and bleak-looking miles of nothing. There was a cement slab out there, which was a good platform for bathing… sort of. I grabbed pitchers out of the kitchen, filled them with water, and had a delightful and desperately needed bucket bath. It was just warm enough and good timing. I could not pedal against that wind, and there would be a Sunday service the next day. After that, the predicted high temperatures would be around 45 degrees. I managed to get done and put everything away before the people showed up for their Saturday music practice.

I was hanging my wash to dry on Truckee when I noticed my first flat tire. 1,780 miles since my departure—not bad. This was as good a time as I could hope for to deal with it. It was a day off, and Truckee was parked in a little area somewhat protected from the wind. I looked and looked in the tire for the culprit that caused the leak, but I could not find anything. The likely suspect was a goathead. These plants grow in dry areas where nothing else will. They have other names such as devil's thorn, devil's weed, and puncturevine—all appropriate.

My first encounter with these things was years ago when I unwittingly rode a borrowed bike across a field in Idaho. Both tires went flat with so many spurs in the wheels that I had to replace both tubes and both tires.

A Samaritan here suggested that if I had to leave the pavement in western Kansas or eastern Colorado, I should carry the bicycle. Well, carrying this bike was not an option for me. Henceforth, I held to the pavement like a soldier, risking life and limb. I would only leave it after careful scrutiny of the terrain. Damned goatheads! The bane of bicycles, dogs, and thinly shod hikers.

After the music practice, I had the good fortune to meet a young man, about 22 years old, who was a jack-of-all-trades farmer/cattleman with a wide variety of interests. He even did computer programming. Oh, and he participated as a living history interpreter at an historic site about 50 miles away. He was a wealth of information about farming and ranching in the area. We talked for hours. Another example of the richness of traveling by bicycle.

I took Truckee down to the gas station to hunt some provisions. I had taken all the panniers off to change the flat tire, so I got to ride without weight. After nearly 2,000 miles of riding loaded, it is such a thrill to ride empty—so fast, so maneuverable! Such a pleasurable break!

There was a farm store adjacent to the convenience store, and I went in there to replace my gloves. I had lost another one of my gloves… again. I re-lost the glove that the nice young lady brought me outside of Dodge City after she saw me drop it.

0 miles.

Day 39 was a Sunday, so when I got out of my sleeping bag, I gussied up in my street outfit. I carry a pair of light pants and an orange shirt that looks almost OK if you shake it out a bit before you need it. The wrinkles slacken after a while. I had used the outfit a few times this trip in the hopes of appearing civilized: Jackson, Tulsa, and now Sheridan Lake. The church had a well-attended, warm Mother's Day service. Every mother received a rose.

After a couple of hours, everyone was gone, and the church was noiseless again except for my ramblings. The man who led the Bible study returned and sat with me a while. He had been a rancher, but now he was a farmer. He was the epitome of pleasant. We talked a long time about that transition from ranching to farming and how either one was a dicey proposition in that arid land. His wife had not attended the service because she was doing 12-hour shifts at an old folks' home. I had no idea where that might be. There was nothing around there. He told me he had nine children. Two were adopted. I wish I could have met his wife. She had to be a saint.

The pastor dropped by later, and we discussed the weather. The outlook wasn't good. A spring storm was a sure thing, and snow was a possibility. He reiterated that I could stay if I needed. It was a wonderful place with wonderful people.

But Toby was getting closer, and I felt a compulsion to get back on the road. I had had two unexpected days off. I would look at the weather in the morning. I at least wanted to get to Eads, 28 miles away. Toby and I could meet there and not have to use up any more of the church's hospitality, though it felt inexhaustible.

0 miles.

When I got up on Day 40, I found that the wind had switched to the southeast and was blowing about 12 miles per hour. That was awesome. It was mostly going to be a tailwind if I broke for Eads. The weather forecasters couldn't seem to decide if it was going to snow or not, but there was consensus that it was going to get lousy.

The sky was heavily overcast. I was hoping this break in the weather was going to last long enough for me to get to Eads. I texted Toby and told him that I would meet him in Eads at some undetermined time and place. I made a reservation at the Cobblestone Inn and Suites where I would wait out the storm. I did not want to spend the night in my tent in whatever Mother Nature was going to come up with now. It was not going to be good.

I wrote as nice a note as I could think of in the guest book at the church and put a wad of money in the donation box. I noted to myself that I was going to send them more if I survived the rest of this trip.

The three-hour ride to Eads went by in a flash. Wide-open country with a tailwind. It was a rolling, dry, and barren landscape. When I got to Eads, I texted Toby. He texted back that he was at the Cenex. It was a gas station that had food and a good-sized sit-down area inside.

I walked in, and the place had a collection of good ol' boys having coffee. It was like the gathering back in Leoti. There were also two loaded XC bicycles outside, and Toby was standing next to a booth engaging the two guys in conversation.

It was especially poignant for me to limp into this place at this time. It was so much fun to see Toby a half a continent away from our homes. I love irony, and this was as ironic as it gets. But add to that running into fellow cyclists riding across the country from the opposite direction.

The two fellows worked together in Georgia not extremely far from where I live. The younger one—around 45 years old—had talked his workmate into this ride. They were thinking about taking a similar ride with some of the troubled youths they worked with. It was a shake-down cruise.

I guess the older guy, 58 years old, had been bemoaning that he was too old for this. When he found out I was 69, he was floored.

We had a great time trading stories of trials and tribulations on the road. Even the good ol' boys got in on the conversation. We laughed and compared travails. These cyclists had woken up one morning to deep snow on their tents. At least I hadn't had that. I told them about getting flooded out in Alabama near where they lived and my near-tornado in Kansas.

Toby had a harrowing experience coming over Wolf Creek Pass on Route 60. The eastern side of the 10,870-foot pass was totally fogged in, and his visor was filming up on the inside as well. There was no place for him to get off the road and automobiles stacked up behind him. He was more than halfway down the slope before he could safely get off the road and let them go by.

We went outside for photo ops, and then Toby took off to the east to try to outrun the weather. I biked with the other guys over to the Traveler's Lodge where they had gotten a room, and then I went to the Cobblestone Inn.

The Cobblestone was described in the literature as two-star and modest. It felt like the lap of luxury to me. I didn't know if I could take that much opulence for two nights, but I'd try. I figured I would have to stay two nights to let the weather run out. I was bummed to be paying $129 per night, but then I got a welcome surprise. They had a bicyclist's rate of $79 per night!

I wheeled my bike into the room way earlier than I normally would be stopping. I gave the television a try. They had a lot of channels, but nothing to watch. The motel had a little, four-stool bar, and I was able to get some food and a beer without having to go out again. Extravagance!

28 miles.

I woke up on Day 41 to see slush on the parked cars outside. It was not going to be a travel day. I had another flat tire as well. I padded down to the continental breakfast and hung out there with coffee. I went back to my room and wrestled all the gear from my bike and turned it upside down. I made a note to myself about how lucky I was to be able to change my second flat tire in a motel room and not outside in the slush somewhere. It was the same tire. Again, I couldn't find anything in the tire that would cause this. I had put a new inner tube on it back at the church. After this, I would only have a patched inner tube for a spare.

This tire was my older tire. The front one was new when I left Florida. I would buy a new tire in Denver and replace this one, but I had to get to Denver. I would get "Slime" in the inner tubes in Denver. 'Slime' is some kind of magic sluice that gets sprayed into the inner tubes and will stop small punctures from leaking as they occur. I called a bike shop in Denver that was near my brother-in-law's house. They assured me that they had the tire I was looking for.

I lazed around the rest of the day in my little slice of splendor.

0 miles.

On Wednesday, May 12, Day 42, I got up for a first light departure. The slush was gone, but there was thick, heavy fog. I had another continental breakfast and lots of coffee, hoping it would lift. I checked out of my room, but then I fell asleep in the lobby waiting for the fog to go away for safer riding. When I awoke from my nap, the fog had lifted enough for me to depart.

I was leaving town on Highway 287, which took me right by the Cenex again. As I was riding, I noticed my shoe had come untied. When I got to the Cenex, I stopped there because they had benches outside. I could sit there to retie my shoe. Luxurious benches! Blessed benches!

I didn't intend to go inside, but as I was tying my shoe, one of the good ol' boys came out and offered to buy me breakfast and coffee. How nice. I went inside and said that I had just had breakfast, but that I would love a coffee. They were interested in more details about my trip, and I had fun providing them with stats and particulars. They joked with one another about who among them was going to ride a bike with me to Denver. I told them I was actually going to Centennial. The guys asked me what route I was taking. I told them I thought I would head straight north to 86 and then head west from there. One of them said Highway 86 was a beautiful road, but hilly. That gave me pause—but not enough. I remembered the guy I met all the way back where I first entered Mississippi. He had warned that the route I was on was "hilly" going toward Jackson, and I eventually had to bail on that route. I would stick with this plan and regret part of it.

CHAPTER 11

Hellish

When I walked out of the Cenex, the streets were still wet, but the fog was gone. I hopped on the bike, and as I was getting onto the road, there was a slight unevenness between the height of the parking lot and the height of the road shoulder. I didn't think anything of it as it was nothing I hadn't encountered before. As I was getting up to speed, I hit it at a shallow angle, and the bike came out from under me. I fell in the road shoulder. The panniers are like buoys, and they kept the bike and my leg off the road. I wasn't injured at all, nor was Truckee, but my self-confidence took a hit. With thousands of miles of experience, I would never have guessed that these circumstances would produce that outcome. I didn't look back to see if anyone saw my accident. I just got back up and continued.

Highway 287 goes straight north, and there was an awesome, 13-MPH wind out of the southeast. The road had rolling hills and lots of truck traffic. But the gradients were shallow, and the road had a perfect road shoulder. I was flying.

After 20 miles, I came to the town of Kit Carson, a town named after a famous frontiersman of the old west. Nevada's capital city, Carson City, had also been named after him. The town felt forsaken to me. I needed to find some water because the next likely services were 40 miles away. I went all the way through town on the highway and found nothing open. I slowly made my way back, looking down the side streets. I rode around behind the volunteer fire department building hoping to find a spigot. Filling my water bottles would be good enough. No luck there.

I continued my backtrack. The Kit Carson Inn had a "No Vacancy" sign, but only the "No" was lit. The bright red "No" loomed mockingly. I thought I might have entered the set of a Clint Eastwood western. I did not see anyone. Maybe I had entered the Twilight Zone. The deserted main road and the red "No" were foreboding.

A block or two later, I saw someone come out of a building on a side street and get in their car. I turned up the street and saw they had come out of a tiny store. There was no sign whatsoever. When I went in, the lady behind the counter said in an even, almost unfriendly voice that I needed a mask. I said that I had one on the bike, but when I turned to get it, she said, "Take one of these," and handed me a free mask. I asked her about filling my water bottles, and she pointed to a sink. I purchased some snacks and left. The desertedness, the no-name store, the coolness of her response to me, and the bright red "No" is how I will always remember Kit Carson, Colorado.

The highway turned northwest, so now the wind was directly behind me. I was in the zone… and I don't mean the Twilight Zone. I was being powered by one of those triple-shot coffee drinks I had purchased at the no-name store.

When I arrived in Hugo, I was hungry, and very happy to find Jean's Family Kitchen open. I ate all the food in the large meal. It was served by a very nice person. When I am at home and eat like that, it inspires a nap. On the road it just fuels more riding.

When I hit the town of Limon, the sun was setting. I topped off my water and got right back on the road. I had to travel nine miles on the Interstate to get to the junction with Highway 86. I knew that on some parts of the Interstate Road System, bicycles are allowed—usually when there are no other choices. I was not certain about this section of Interstate 70, but I was going to get on it and find out. I would have to travel a long way out of my way if it wasn't permitted, and that is the point of allowing bicycles on some parts of the Interstate Road System. There were no prohibition signs on the ramp, so I figured I was good to go. Again, it felt like permission.

Traveling on the Interstate shoulder is probably safer than most other roads. Just like back on the Muskogee Turnpike, the cyclist has a 10-foot-wide lane with a rumble strip on the traffic side of it. The main problem with riding the Interstate Highway is that it is not pleasant. The frequent if not crowded traffic is noisy. I carry earplugs for these occasions, but they only temper the din. Also, the Interstate shoulders are usually strewn with exploded truck tires and their steel belts.

I had my tailwind all the way to the junction with Highway 86. Another reason I wanted to get there is that my wind app said the wind was coming around to westerly. It was going to be the end of my glorious tailwind for a while.

There was nothing at this intersection. The choices were to go west on 86 or get back on the Interstate. There was a county road headed east that turned to a dirt surface right away on its way to nowhere.

It was ominous that GMB did not give Highway 86 as an option for going to Centennial. The two options it gave were going way out of the way to the northwest through Aurora or farther out of the way to the southwest through Colorado Springs. Highway 86 went straight west toward my destination. Tomorrow, I might find a reason that GMB did not recommend or even acknowledge this route, but for tonight, it would remain a mystery.

This highway cloverleaf was a pigpen. I had not been exposed to this amount of litter in a long while. After a wearisome day of riding, I set my tent up just out of the cloverleaf and away from the litter. It was dark by the time I got in it. I thought about how lucky I had been with weather and hideouts. It had been perfectly nice crossing Kansas with highs in the mid-60s. It was near freezing a couple times further south, but this had been perfect. The snow yesterday renewed my unease about having left Florida too early, so that now I might hit snowstorms in the western states.

I was within earshot of Interstate 70, but the noise wasn't terrible. I could not have gone further down Highway 86 because darkness had overtaken me. I reflected on that magnificent tailwind I had all day.

93 miles.

I woke early to dense fog and heavy dew. It had not rained, but everything was soggy wet. My rainfly and the tent were wet. Even my sleeping bag was dank. I balled everything into the panniers and left. Somewhere down the road, I would take a break and dry everything out as was my habit after mornings like this. Normally, I pick up litter around a stealth camp, but this amount of refuse was overwhelming. I couldn't have carried it all or even made a dent in it.

I embarked on Highway 86 west. Not much shoulder, but not much traffic. It was hilly as the guy back in Eads tried to tell me. Too hilly. Maybe this was why GMB didn't list it as an option. Or maybe it was the wind. Did GMB know that the wind on this road would always be in an eastbound cyclist's face? I would guess that it was at least nine MPH and almost head-on. There would be no services until Kiowa 36 miles away. Under average conditions, I would not have thought much of that, but now I was struggling. After only seven miles, I pulled off the road and draped my tent, rainfly, and sleeping bag over the guard rail to dry. The fog was long gone, and now it was sunny, adding heat to my list of tribulations along with hills and headwinds.

On my first cross-country trip, I had passed through the "Texas Hill Country." It was beautiful. But it was a seemingly endless series of parabolas, none of which could I top without getting off Truckee and pushing. It might have been fun on an empty bike, but for me with my heavy gear, it was torment. At least there I came to a crossroad that led me to a larger, flatter four-lane highway.

I consulted GMB to see if there was possibly a way out this time. The long way was looking good right now. There was one, final option, but it was a dirt road, and I didn't want to add that to the list of adversities.

I packed my stuff and got going again. The wind would not relent nor would the hills. In fact, the hills seemed to be getting more pronounced. Or was I just wearing down? More work meant drinking more water over a shorter distance. It became clear that my water was not going to last until Kiowa.

The scattered farmhouses were mostly far off the road. I could ride out and ask them for water, but I didn't want to risk going that far out of my way to find no one home.

I came upon a house that was right next to the road, and there was a man parked in front of it with his engine running. I rode up to him, and he rolled down his window with a very unwelcoming look. I asked him if he had any water to spare, and he said no—that he needed it for his daughter. I suddenly realized that he did not belong to the house. He had just pulled over there to get his daughter sorted out. He was going through some ordeal of his own. I'm sure that I was exactly the inconvenience he acted like I was. He left in a hurry. I looked at the house, and it looked like no one was around, so I left too.

A little bit later, I was stopped at the top of a hill for a break, and a sheriff's deputy pulled up behind me. He asked if I was alright. I told him I was fine but that I was almost out of water. He gave me what water he had. He said his shift was done and that he would tell the next guy to watch out for me. I'm not sure what that meant, but at least now I had more water.

The water did not last long. Maybe GMB didn't suggest this route because it knew that you couldn't possibly carry enough water on a bicycle to make the transit.

I was struggling along when one of those giant bus campers rode past from the other direction and the driver threw something out the window that hit me right in the chest. I think it was gum. It happened fast, but I could see the driver was a man 50 years old or older. Let's call him Caligula.

When cycling across the country, one can be exposed to far worse things than having gum thrown at them. Fortunately, it doesn't happen very often. You have poor Caligula driving a vehicle that is valued at more than my net worth getting bored and deciding it would be fun to try and hit this guy struggling on his bike. Score! Direct hit! Caligula 1, cyclist 0.

We all age, but some never mature. Why is that? Some dissolve into self-pity, some fall into deranged seriousness, some just try to outdo whomever they can compare themselves to. These are all manifestations of unseen and unchecked ego—baby Caligulas aged into adults. I hope that someone like Caligula would stop at a childish prank, but it seems unlikely. This person was clearly unhappy.

Part of the problem is that we are not taught at an early age, nor are most of us ever exposed to the fact that we cause our own unhappiness. This has been an open secret for a few thousand years, but some might only be hearing it now for the first time. When I first heard of this, I was disbelieving also. We can start with a kind of facile example and perhaps work up to larger things.

Caligula hits me with his gum. I have a choice about how I react and how long I hold on to the incitement. I can react by, say, flipping him off. That is not much less juvenile, but it is an option. In this case, probably the only option I have for voicing my displeasure to him. Then, I can hold onto my anger about the incident for as long as I want.

It is my own anger that I want to address here. Caligula? Well, something in his life made him pathetic enough to do that. It isn't the point. He can justify his actions to his grave. But if I carry anger about something like this for any distance, I am only damaging me. And then, I might possibly pass that bad energy along in some impertinent behavior that damages people I encounter.

This is the essence of karma. People in the "West" think that karma is some magical thing. That explanation of karma never worked for me. I didn't want to have to believe in something that is not experiential. Years ago at university, I did an independent study on Buddhism. I had stumbled upon a translation of an ancient text in which the author said karma simply meant action. No magic. One action leads to another.

You wake up in a foul mood, and you go to work and yell at your employee. He goes home and beats his wife, which deepens her depression.

You wake up in a good mood and go to work and give your employee a raise. He goes home and takes his spouse out for dinner, and they go home and make love.

You can follow either of these situations until they peter out. That is the karmic wheel. There is nothing to believe in here. It is seeable by everyone. No magic. Everyone can see constant examples of this in their own lives. The question becomes can you see these effects in your own life both coming and being passed along. You must see these causes and effects in YOURSELF before you can affect the continuum. It is a matter of some vigilant observation of yourself before you will start enhancing the positive continuum and bringing an end to the bad karma. Most of us just absorb a stimulus and then react, and then think we are justified.

In this example Caligula is just passing along barely perceived slights without enough self-awareness to intercede. He cannot stop himself because he cannot see himself.

After I rode a while completely out of water, I found a long, flat straightaway in the road between two hills. This was going to be my last stand. I stopped in the middle between the hills. It was open enough for people in either direction to see me and stop safely. And then, hopefully, for other motorists to see anyone who stopped for me.

I stood on the road shoulder holding an empty water bottle upside down as each car passed. I did not have to wait long. Six or eight cars passed in each direction before a fellow in a pickup truck pulling an empty horse trailer pulled over on my side of the road. At the very same time, a guy who had spotted me while traveling in the other direction made a U-turn and joined us. Between the two of them, they left me with all the water I could carry and some cold Gatorade.

Water problem solved, but that still left me with the other banes: the wind and the hills. Kiowa was closer now, but the hills were still daunting, and the wind was torturous. It was bad enough trying to pedal up the hills against the wind, but sometimes I had to pedal downhill against the wind.

I crossed a long valley with gentler rises, which ended at a hill that had to be a half a mile long. I could barely pedal to the beginning of it. I resigned myself to walking the bicycle the entire way to the top. It took me a long time with lots of breaks. As I was nearing the top, a very fit young man stopped his car at the crest and ran down to me. He grabbed the bike to walk it to the top, but I had to stop him so I could get my cane. Without Truckee or a cane to lean on, I couldn't have gone even one step up or down that rise.

When I caught up to him at the top, he said that he thought the bike might have been broken. I told him, no, the bike wasn't broken, but I was. He offered to give me and Truckee a lift. I thanked him, but told him I'd have to pass, that I was determined to make the trip without rides. He understood. He said Kiowa was five or six miles farther. He told me that crossing the hills at Comanche Creek would be challenging and then Wolf Creek and then I would be there.

One more thing about karma. It can be stored. We store it in our minds—or more precisely our psyches—and this stored karma is what feeds our desires and our fears. All of them. If you get bitten by a dog, it is possible you will feel a fear of dogs for the rest of your life. In the case of baby Caligula, he might see someone getting something that he does not and carry some measure of that resentment his entire life. A therapist might look for that early action (karma) that caused him such anxiety in his life with the hopes of pointing it out to him. When he can see it, there is the possibility to let it go. Until then, he is likely to pass his anxiety on to everyone he encounters. In his discussions about the "pain body," Eckhart Tolle examines this stored karma beautifully.

I rolled into Kiowa in the afternoon. The 36 miles since I left the littered cloverleaf had taken nine hours. That was slow even for a guy who wasn't in a hurry.

I stopped in the High Plains Food Store and did not see anything I wanted. After my ordeal, I wanted to sit somewhere and order food served to me. I needed to not move for a while and sit on something besides my bicycle—no offense, Truckee.

A customer struck up a conversation with me about my trip. I asked her if she could recommend a place to eat in town, and she said Patty Ann's. I also asked if she knew of anyplace to camp. She said there was the Fawn Valley Park, but she wasn't sure if camping was allowed there.

So, I went to Patty Ann's and found it to be just what I needed. I was pleasantly served a big pile of food, which I devoured.

Now I was ready to get a beer to have at my campsite. I rode over to the Sinclair Station convenience store, but they didn't have any beer. I asked what was up, hoping it wasn't a dry county. The guy said no. They couldn't sell beer in convenience stores; you had to go to a liquor store. He directed me to MK Liquors.

There was still a lot of daylight left, so I crazily decided to make my way toward Elizabeth, Colorado about seven miles away. I hoped I could find a good stealth camp along the way, but that wasn't to be. On top of that, it was a very hilly seven miles.

One of the first things I came to at Elizabeth was Casey Jones Park. It was the kind of park that closes at sundown so camping would not be permitted. It was wooded, but kind of wide open. It would have been difficult to be stealthy.

I went out of the park the back way to explore further and came upon a huge Latter-day Saints church that was oriented perfectly for hiding. As I went around the building to make camp, I spooked a mule deer—a very good indicator that this was likely a rarely disturbed spot.

As I was getting settled in, I went slightly around the back corner of the church, and there was a fenced-in dog watching me. I could tell he had already detected me, but he remained silent and patiently waited for me to show myself. Thankfully, he didn't let out a peep. My tent was already set up, and I didn't want to attract attention. The dog just stared at me. I waved at him and went back to my tent. Around 9 p.m., a misty rain started but ended quickly.

Day 43 had been grueling, but it ended well in a nice spot near a nice dog.

43 miles.

I slept very well and woke up just before the sunrise. I broke camp and peeked around the corner to see if Quiet Dog was out. He wasn't. I sent thanks to him.

I was targeting a coffee shop that was not going to be open until 7:30, but on the way I stumbled upon Isabel's Coffee, which was already open. I've routinely found that when one types in a search—say, coffee shop—you get a selection, but not necessarily all that are available.

I had an excellent coffee there and a breakfast burrito. I texted Tom and Becky in Centennial and told them I would likely make it to their house in the afternoon. Tom is my wife's brother. I told them, as I was leaving Tulsa, that I was headed to Denver, and they offered to put me up. Since then, I had been "pinging" them along the way with updated estimates of my arrival time.

GMB had suggested an excellent route from Elizabeth, so I knew it was only going to be a 35-mile ride today. I was happy to note that Elizabeth was higher in elevation than Centennial, so I would be averaging downhill by 746 feet. While I was breakfasting in Isabel's, a guy came in with spurs on his boots. I had yet to see that though I had traveled at length through horse-and-cow country.

My thoughts returned to the deer I saw last night. For some reason, I had not seen that many deer on this trip though I had traveled through beautiful deer habitat.

On my first cross-country trip, I had a distressing deer incident in east Texas.

I was on a two-lane road with no shoulder and no traffic. It was an excellent road with not much going on except for great scenery. At one point up ahead, I saw seven deer milling across the road from right to left. As I neared where they had been, I saw two more deer running parallel to the road on my side—evidently along a wire fence.

An SUV appeared oncoming, traveling very fast. I only had time to think to the deer, "Don't do it!" I figured they were running from me, and at the end of the fence, they would try to join their buddies. We converged right where I had seen the first seven deer. The two stragglers bolted across the road like lightning. The first deer made it by inches, and the second deer got creamed right in the center of the SUV grill. I watched the deer come off the front of the car and slide in the road. I was close enough that little bits of the car's grill fell on me as momentum carried me past.

The vehicle came to a stop, but it was leaking fluids. It was too damaged to drive very far. The lady driving got out of the car and exclaimed, "I just got my car out of the shop from hitting a deer!"

I don't know if she rides around harvesting deer with her car, but I do know that in this case she did not have one second to react. And I am sure that the deer was dead before it finished its slide.

She opened the back door of the car to check on her two girls safely buckled into their car seats. I walked over to see if I could be of help. The lady told me that as the accident happened, she was afraid the deer might come off the car and hit me.

I noticed that in that big SUV the small children weren't high enough in their car seats to see anything, so they didn't have to witness that. The driver got on her phone to call Grandma to come and get the girls while she dealt with the stricken car. The older of the two children was about four years old. She asked me if the deer was dead. I don't know how to smooth things with small children, and out came the truth, "Yes." Then she asked me if it was a boy deer. I said, "No, it was a girl deer." She didn't seem to be upset whichever the possibility. I asked her if she was alright, and she said yes in a beautiful, friendly way.

I dragged the deer out of the road and asked the mom if I could help further. I told her I had water and snacks if needed. She said she was fine and that help was on its way.

There was more hill-and-dale getting west of Elizabeth on the dreaded Highway 86, but then I rocketed down to Franktown. Beautiful day, wind in my face, not having to pedal. An XC cyclist's dream. Even though the downhill ended, the pleasure did not. Just west of Franktown, I got on the Cherry Creek Trail. What a beautiful resource! From there I traveled almost exclusively on bike trails all the way to my brother-in-law's house. This trail followed Cherry Creek, so I did not even have to intersect with cars. The roads crossed the creek on bridges, and the trail stayed down along the creek under the roads. The trail was nice and wide and well used on this lovely day. That is as good as it gets for biking in civilization.

Of course, it couldn't stay perfect, and GMB can't know about every construction site on the bike paths, so I did have to ford a small creek where a bike bridge was out. Fording saved me having to find roads around the obstruction, which can be very tedious. Especially since GMB just keeps insisting you to take the bridge that isn't there and refuses to make another suggestion.

It was great to arrive at Tom and Becky's. They generously allotted half of the two-car garage to me so I could park the bike in the middle of my half and unload the panniers and spread out all my stuff. This was a big stop for me. I needed to fine-tune all my equipment for the remainder of the trip. I assumed I was about halfway by distance, but I had no way of knowing for sure since I did not have a definitive route.

Truckee needed to see the doctor. I had to replace that worn tire and the chain, and possibly the rear sprocket cluster. I would ask at the bike shop what else they could think of. I still had more than 1,800 miles to go.

35 miles.

The next day, I biked over to the shop I had called to order a new tire. I met with disappointment there as there was a misunderstanding and they did NOT have the tire that I had called about. Nor did they have anything that was close to what I needed.

This is a situation that would have caused me a lot of angst in my earlier years. Now that I realize that I am 100 percent responsible for my feelings and reaction, it is not a bother. I had called about a specific tire and size, which the person I talked to thought they had. He was wrong. Spouting off never helps. Never! "So, now what?" is the only reasonable response. Getting angry or upset ADDS NOTHING! It just creates bad karma. We tend to add story at this point. It is important to see this: "I was counting on this tire; I have been led astray; they are stupid; they are irresponsible; this is a shitty bike shop." If you can catch yourself doing this, you are well on the way to discovering a beautiful peace that is always available within. A peace that you can pass on. Once you develop this equanimity, you are not going to pass on the internally generated suffering. It takes time to see this, but it is worth the effort—for yourself and everyone you encounter. You are not Caligula.

I asked them if they could recommend another bicycle shop where I might find what I was looking for. They kindly recommended two.

The second bike shop I went to was gigantic. But in the Denver area, cyclists are more into road biking and mountain biking. In the simplest terms, road bikes use skinny tires for speed, less friction, and aerodynamics. Mountain bikers use fat knobby tires for stability and durability on tough trails. Touring bikes use something kind of in the middle. A road bike tire is usually about 1" in diameter. Mountain bike tires are often 2.2" to nearly 3" in diameter and have deep tread. I run 2" diameter tires but with very little tread. 1.5" or 1.75" would be a little faster, but I seem to often end up on dirt roads, and I like 2" for better stability if that befalls me.

The second bike shop did not have exactly what I was looking for in a tire either. Something about COVID had made many bicycle parts harder to come by. Bicycle sales increased during the pandemic, so parts were in increased demand.

I rolled on to the third shop. It was also gigantic. The fellow helping me was also a bike mechanic. He disappeared back into the inventory and found that they also did not have exactly what I wanted. He brought out three other options. I chose to go with a 1.75" diameter road tire. It was close enough to the 2" that I wanted, and I asked him to mount it on the front. The back tire carries more weight and consequently takes more abuse from the road. Had I left Florida with two equivalent tires, I would just have had them swapped front to back—a bicycle tire rotation. But when I left Florida, I had one new tire and one worn tire. I was now replacing the worn one. I wanted to keep the wider tire on the back.

While he was looking over the bike, he squeezed one of the brake levers, and the cable broke! I have never said I am not lucky. For the cable to break in the bike shop is too serendipitous to be true. I thanked Truckee for that bit of foresight.

The fellow inspired confidence in me. I listed a few things I wanted done, and then I told him to do whatever he would do if he had to get 2,000 miles out of this bicycle. I left it with him and walked over to a nearby brewery in search of a dark beer.

After a beer and some finger food, I strolled back to the bike shop. He was still working on my bike, so I stood in the work room and talked to the three mechanics that were all working on bikes. We talked a lot about biking in Colorado. Denver is in close proximity to excellent mountain biking trails. I used to do a lot of it, but I have aged out of it. It was fun to take lots of risks when I was younger, but now I just feel too brittle for it. I don't fall nearly as much on my touring bike, and I am a lot more judicious with the brakes than I used to be. I don't hurry down hills because it is that much sooner to have to pedal up. Why waste a good coast?

I was extremely pleased when I left the bike shop. With the new chain and sprocket cassette and all the adjustments, it felt like I was riding a new bicycle. The inner tubes were filled with a sealant that automatically patches the tube from the inside if there is a small puncture. I could be a little less cautious about goathead spurs or sand spurs. It is pretty much a necessity in the western states, though Florida has a pretty nasty sand spur as well. I biked back to the house and was happy to be indoors on a bed for the night.

9 miles.

Day 46 of the bicycle odyssey was completely a day of leisure. I didn't touch the bike or even look at it. I had a great time just visiting with my hosts. I actually rode in the car a few times! It was an odd pleasure after not having been in a vehicle since Tulsa back on Day 29.

Tom stopped at an Army Navy store for something, and while I was looking around, I found a tarp that was the length of my tent and half again as wide. I thought I would use it to replace my rain poncho, which I had damaged severely when I dragged my bike on it under the culvert escaping the near tornado.

This turned out to be much better suited for a ground cloth, and it was very light. The dual purpose of the rain poncho being a ground cloth was just one of my bargain-basement-inspired ideas that did not pan out. I had found that wearing a rain poncho did not work well on my touring bike.

0 miles.

Day 47 was a leisurely day also. I biked around taking care of some business odds and ends. I also went back to the bike shop to get some Schrader/Presta valve adapters. The hand air pump I carry in my tool bag is designed to work on either valve type. The Schrader valve is the most common valve in the United States. All cars and lots of bicycles have this kind of valve. But a lot of bicycles, including mine, have Presta valves. You have probably seen these skinnier valves. They are much better valves for the high-pressure tires that you see on many road and racing bikes. The problem comes if you have to use a gas station air pump. I have never seen one that can accommodate a Presta valve, so I wanted to have an adapter on each tire.

Another problem that an XC cyclist should be warned about is those coin-operated tire pumps that have taken over. Most car tires inflate to 30 pounds PSI or so. That is what these machines are designed for. My bicycle tires are designed for 55 to 70 pounds of pressure, and some of the coin ops won't go that high. It is possible to try to inflate your tire and lose PSI. I prefer for mine to be 65 to 70 PSI for more efficiency. Softer tires are less efficient. More work per mile.

20 miles.

CHAPTER 12

The Perfect Storm

On Day 48, I timed my departure with Tom's leaving for work. They had made me feel very comfortable, and I had such an enjoyable visit it was tempting to stay longer. But I had accomplished all my mid-trip goals, and I felt antsy to continue the odyssey. Despite possible rain, I said my goodbyes and departed.

I was headed toward Wyoming via Fort Collins, Colorado. My next major goal was Missoula, Montana. I wanted to stop at the Adventure Cycling Association's Headquarters. But that was about 900 miles away. A route had not come to mind yet.

The ACA maps and lots of cyclists route through Jackson, Wyoming and Yellowstone National Park. Those are fabulously beautiful, stunning places that I was pretty sure I wanted to avoid. I am fortunate to have been to both several times by vehicle. I would suggest to people who have never been to go there by any means. But tourist season would soon be underway, and the thought of my slow ass on those hills and curves with no shoulder was stultifying. Tourist camper vehicles seem to be getting bigger and bigger and bigger. And even in a place as beautiful as Yellowstone, there are always plenty of people in as big a hurry as ever. Possibly even a few Caligulas. Nope. I didn't want to die under the wheels of somebody in a rush to see Old Faithful's next eruption. I was sidestepping one of the most exquisite places in the United States. I just hadn't figured out how I was going to go about it.

The side benefit of making my own route northwest was going to be covering territory that I have never seen before and will likely never see again. That is something that biking, and bike routes, are all about.

GMB did not let me down going north through the greater Denver area. It suggested mostly bike paths with beautiful windings along Cherry Creek and the South Platte River.

It started to rain outside of Broomfield, and I found a Starbucks to hide in. It was not a drencher, but a very light chilly rain that would have soaked me in no time. I was trying to avoid putting on my rain gear. It took time to get it on, and it is warm to ride in. Then there was having to take it off and repack it wet. I probably spent an hour in the coffee shop.

There were good roads and bike paths the whole way. Longmont had a nice feel to it, and in Loveland the bike path followed along the Big Thompson River. Then Highway 15 took me along Lake Loveland. There was a wonderful bike path along South Shield Street, but it was getting late, and I was going to need to find a hideout. I had looked for a possibility coming out of Loveland, a church, a copse. Nothing presented itself.

The bike path leading into Fort Collins went through some nice terrain, but it was wide open. I could tell that this was not going to be ideal. Finally, I stopped in a high area along the bike path that was open: no trees, no nothing. The weeds weren't even very high. I waited until just before dark to set up my tent. A few late pedestrians went by, and I just waved and said hello. Nobody seemed worried, and I couldn't have gone further anyway. I was tired. I would just have to make a first-light departure. The positive side of this non-stealthy camp was that I had a great vantage point for a gorgeous sunset.

85 miles.

When I woke up in the morning, everything was soaked with dew. I packed up as it was getting light, and I knew that I would have to unpack for a period of drying later. I stopped for breakfast at the First Watch Breakfast along Highway 287. This was a highway that I was going to become quite familiar with. I had eaten at a First Watch in Sarasota, Florida, but until now, I did not know they were a chain. They had very healthy choices that would normally be out of my budget, but I thought this would be the first restaurant that my wife would have approved of on this whole trip. She is a very healthy eater, and I know she would hate XC cycling if only for the very limited choices of healthy food. She would eschew the food and coffee at most of my stops and would starve to death before finishing the trip.

I had a heck of a time getting the rest of the way out of Colorado. The elevation changes after leaving Centennial were mild. Between there and Fort Collins, there is a drop of around 800 feet. In a car it would have felt flat. But now I would be climbing up and out of Colorado toward Laramie, Wyoming. Highway 287 travels up along the Owl Creek drainage. By the time I had gotten to The Forks diner outside of Livermore, Colorado, I had gained 900 feet. I was very happy to see this place because it would be the last of services for quite some time. It was large enough to have some inside seating, which was welcoming. They had good, made-to-order food and a curio shop, and the staff was very friendly. I filled all my water bottles and my Camelback bladder. Even though the town of Virginia Dale shows up on the map, I was warned that there would be no services until Laramie. I was about 41 miles from Laramie, and I would be gaining over 1,200 more feet in elevation. I would encounter a lot of slow traveling ahead. Thus far, I had been able to top all the climbs without getting off the bike. I had spent quite a bit of time in gears one and two with some nice drops in elevation in-between. However, I knew that every drop had to be reclaimed. It could take a little fun out of it if you let it.

It was beautiful, dry country, and the average high temperature at this time of year was in the low 60s. The average low was below 40 degrees. That is good going-up-hill temperature and excellent sleeping condition at night. When you factor in wind, though, efforts can change radically. At this point the wind was not influencing me much. I was winding in different directions, and the wind was mildly out of the west.

I came to Virginia Dale at the top of a long climb. Sure enough, there was a boarded-up building that must have been a diner in the distant past. Evidently, the place was established as a stage stop along the Overland Trail back in the mid-1800s. It even had a hotel back then. The stagecoach could be held up by inclement weather, and there had to be somewhere for passengers to rest. A character named Jack Slade was the manager back in the late 1800s, and he had quite a reputation both as a good manager and a miscreant. Samuel Clemens met him and described him as a desperado when he published *Roughing It* in 1872 under the pen name Mark Twain. By then Mr. Slade had been hanged by angry miners in Virginia City, Montana.

Nowadays, there is just this closed café/post office with a sign that looks like it was made in the 1950s. It was five miles to the Wyoming border.

I crossed into Wyoming under mostly cloudy skies. Depending on which way I looked, it seemed that rain was a possibility. But if it did rain, it would be the kind where I rode under a heavy downpour and then out again. I still had some climbing to do as I would reach 8,000 feet in elevation before I started a long descent into Laramie.

The hills started leveling out as the toughest part fell behind me. It felt good to get to ride in flatter country again. Good road continued with good shoulder. The traffic wasn't bad, but everyone seemed to be in an even bigger hurry to get across the nothingness. It was wide-open terrain again.

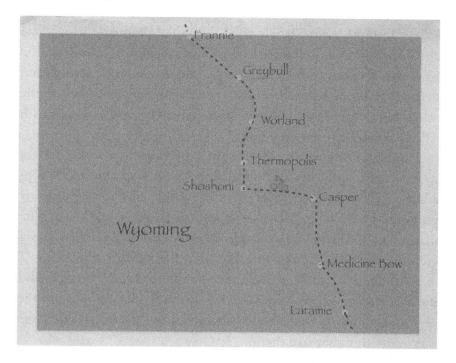

I cruised into Laramie just before dark. Just outside of town, some highway patrolmen rolled alongside me. There was no traffic at this point, and we had a conversation as we kept moving. They had seen me way the hell back there and were impressed by my progress. They were very impressed when I told them I had ridden there from Florida and that this was Day 49. Nice guys.

I took a room at the Travelodge. It had been two long days of high mileage. I had to find some paper maps, and having a room to leave the panniers in while I rode around town was essential. Laramie is a college town, and I was hoping for some good bookstores that would have maps.

75 miles.

I slept in until 8 a.m. It felt good. I secured permission for a late checkout and then rode over to the Chuckwagon for breakfast. The place was very busy. I ordered a veggie omelet with hash browns and toast. Back home I would choose one carbohydrate and pass on the other. But riding these kinds of distances, hash browns and toast with jelly is allowable if not necessary.

I rode across town to the Walmart hoping they would have a selection of maps. They had none in the book/magazine area except atlases. As I mentioned, atlas pages are not detailed enough for my purposes. I went to the automotive section, and they had lots of state maps… all of Colorado! I went outside and called the Laramie County Community College bookstore, but they did not deal in maps.

With fingers crossed, I called the Grand Newsstand, but they did not stock maps either. I asked if they had any suggestions, and the very nice-sounding woman said I should try the Visitor's Center. She was pretty sure they had them.

As luck would have it, the Visitor's Center was map Mecca. I picked up maps for Wyoming, Montana, and Idaho. The only other map I would need was Washington State, but I would have to get that elsewhere. This was a very exciting find. More so because they gave you the maps for free. Hallelujah!

During earlier planning, I had purchased the Adventure Cycling Association maps for getting from Rawlins, Wyoming to Astoria, Oregon and had them sent to my brother-in-law's house in Centennial. Those maps cover the western third of the TransAmerica Bicycle Route. By now, however, I knew I did not want to go through Yellowstone, nor did I want to end up in Astoria. I took the five maps over to The Pedal House bicycle shop and donated them. I didn't need to carry them anymore, and I figured someone there would find them interesting if not useful. I had a great time discussing cycling there, and the mechanic had done some long-distance, overnight bike journeys. I felt vindicated when he told me he carried two sleeping mats also. He was quite a bit younger than me.

I went back to the motel and packed. I vacated the room and stopped for lunch at a grocery store. I was also able to get a giant iced coffee for the ride. It was an unusually late start to my riding day, but there was a wind out of the southeast at 15 to 20 MPH. Perfect. And it was downhill to Medicine Bow by about 600 feet of elevation—also perfect.

I rode inspired. I had my maps, I had my iced coffee, I had my tailwind. I was not drifting along the high plains, I was rocketing. At one point going down a long slope with wind pushing, I did 31 MPH for two miles—a remarkable joy. The road was good, and the traffic was sparse.

I stopped at a convenience store in Rock River, but I didn't really want to get off the bike. The wind was still blowing hard and gusting up dust. Still, I thought I should grab a snack and fill my water. There was an old guy at the counter. When I told him I was from Florida, he said he wintered in Fort Myers, Florida. Small world.

I was back on the road in no time, pedaling hard and still excited by the energizing wind. It seemed to be slowing down a little and coming more easterly as I arrived in Medicine Bow. It started sprinkling a little, and as I got to JB's gas station, it started pouring rain. I was not in the rain for very long, but I got quite wet. I grabbed some food and stood around inside until the rain quit. The guy behind the counter assured me that there would be no services between Medicine Bow and Casper—89 miles. I filled my Camelback bladder. You want to have water when you need it, but you don't want to carry it if you don't have to. It is heavy.

My relationship with Highway 287 was coming to an end. I would be turning northward on Wyoming 487. Before I got to my turn, I passed the Virginian Hotel. It is a sight that you would not expect to see in this small town. A three-and-a-half story block hotel that was built in 1911 in Italian Renaissance style. It reminded me of coming upon the huge monastery back in Subiaco, Arkansas. This was not as large, but it was equally unexpected.

As I turned onto 487, I came upon a sign that said, "Rest Area Closed Ahead." I had not known that there was a rest area ahead, so I was not as disappointed as I might have been. The wind was no longer blowing from behind me. It was on my side. I had really gotten to enjoy some favorable wind, which made for a high mileage day despite my late start.

I rode another 18 miles before stopping for the night. I did not pull very far off the road to set up my tent. It wasn't necessary. There was no cover, but very little traffic. There would likely be no traffic over night anyway. It looked like the rain had given up too. As I lay there, I marveled at my mileage over the last three days. 82.5 miles per day even with today's late start.

88 miles.

I slept very well and woke up to 39 degrees. I leisurely broke camp and got back on the road. No hot coffee in my future today. I had developed the habit of buying a canned coffee beverage the day before to have on mornings like this. When I got back on the road, it was clear that the glorious tailwind was over. It had been replaced with about a four-MPH headwind. Same trip, different wind. It was a cinch that I would not make it to Casper today.

As the day wore on, the cloud cover went from complete overcast to partly cloudy, but the wind stepped up to about eight MPH in my face. I don't think the temperature got above the low 40s. For a long time, I was in sight of a giant wind farm with tall towers. It mocked me as it ceaselessly pointed out that the wind was indeed against me.

A constant reminder. Yes, I felt it. I was glad that someone somewhere was getting some electricity from my ardor.

Another disappointment came when, about halfway along my Highway 487 journey, I came upon the purported rest area. Not only was it not closed, but it had running water and flush toilets! It was a very clean building that was designed to use passive solar. It was a little oasis of modernity in the very middle of nowhere. I had carried a lot of extra water—against the wind—for nothing.

The weather was starting to look threatening. 487 had turned straight west, and in some number of miles, I was going to hit Wyoming 220 that would take me north into Casper. The area was more settled but still very spare. I had seen a lot of pronghorn antelope, but now I was seeing a few horses again. I stopped along the road to reconnoiter. There were five horses about 300 yards away across a giant paddock. The area was vast, and I could see long distances. There were places around me where I could see rain falling. I really didn't want to get wet now. The temperature was still in the 40s, and the wind made it more uncomfortable. Such a difference between this day's cold, arduous ride and yesterday's screaming delight. I contemplated putting on my rain gear, but I wasn't smart enough to follow through with it. It was late afternoon, and I was more than 20 miles from Casper. I wasn't going to make it there, so I had to find a camp.

I looked up from my phone and map to see that the five horses had crossed the field and were standing at the fence staring at me. I don't know anything about horses, but these were beautiful. The one on the left was light brown with a black mane. The next one was very dark brown also with a black mane, and a white stripe down the middle of its face. The third one was dark brown with a brown mane and a thin white stripe on its face. The fourth one was all white. The one on the right was light tan with a black mane and black legs. They were all a picture of health. I was pleased that they had bothered to come all the way across the field to see what I was up to. Charming.

I got back on the bike sans rain gear to see how far I could get. I probably rode six or seven miles when it began to rain. I was pretty much caught in the open. I could see a farmhouse and barn up ahead, and I made for it. The opening to the property was on the barn side. I would have stopped at the house for permission, but I was getting in trouble. My light riding jacket was quite wet, and I was getting cold. I ducked into the giant barn and pulled up next to a stack of hay bales. I leaned Truckee against a post right by the doorway and pulled out my heavier jacket and my down sleeping bag. I put the jacket on and then huddled under the bag around the corner from the doorway. I was cold, but I was thankful to be out of the wind and rain. The strong smell of hay added a measure of comfort.

Someone must have seen me go into the barn because after a bit, a vehicle pulled into the entrance I had used. They only pulled in a little way and stopped. They could see my loaded bicycle, but they could not see me behind the bales. I started to unbury myself, but they pulled back out and left.

I was in the barn for half an hour. By then it had stopped raining, and I had warmed up. I thought about rolling over to the house and thanking them for their presumed hospitality, but it was quite a way. The driveway was now muddy and rutted. I figured if they had really wanted to speak to me, they would have disembarked the vehicle. I pushed the bike back up to the road and pedaled on.

I was seeing nowhere to set up my tent and nothing in the way of shelter. There was a school bus stop along the road, but I didn't think I could stretch out in it, and it looked like it might have been on private property. I was hoping there would be something at the intersection with Highway 220. Given the lay of the land, it was a major intersection.

The junction provided no clear opportunities. There was some kind of farm supply place that was closed and fenced in. It was a T intersection with nothing in either direction. There was a house across the road and a metal shed type of building that might have been on the same property but was not next to the house. With the encroaching darkness, I was not going to get much farther, so I thought I'd just go ask for help. I could ask at the house for permission to spend the night in the shed. If it wasn't theirs, maybe they would know who I could call and ask.

As I approached the house, I could tell that it was not occupied, nor had anyone driven on the road up to it for quite some time. Perhaps it was a seasonal house. At any rate, I wasn't going to approach it. I would look in the shed first. There were no vehicle tracks around the shed, and the sliding door was ajar. I peeped in and could see that it was used to store machinery. The stuff inside was covered in thick dust. There were no tracks in the dust inside either. The man-door at the front of the building was not locked.

No one had been here for a long time. There was a sizable tear in the metal roofing, which brought in the loess. I liked nothing about the place except that it would give me shelter from the elements for one night. It was very windy by now, and I decided to stay there. It was close to dark, and I couldn't have gotten but a few more miles down the road anyway. I brought Truckee inside and spread out my tarp. After that, I stayed on the tarp for the rest of the night. I didn't want to get talc-like dust on any of my stuff, nor did I want to inhale it. I can't say that I was comfortable, but at least I was out of the sporadic rain and strong wind. My weather app registered 39 degrees, and my wind app indicated the wind at 16 MPH NNE. Thank goodness I was out of it… more or less.

58 miles.

This was going to be a special day though I didn't know it. The ride up to Casper was grueling. First thing, the temperature was 32 degrees.

Too cold to ride in the headwind, but I couldn't spend any more time in the dust shack. There was new snow in the low mountains nearby. I was 19 miles from Casper. It would take me hours, but I promised myself a motel room when I got there. The latest weather was taking its toll on me. After a while, it felt like the whole ride was uphill, but it couldn't have been. Highway 220 follows along the North Platte River downstream. I suppose it was the headwind and the hills the road took to get away from the river. It was very beautiful, and it would have been great to see it under more favorable conditions.

Those moments where beauty can take your mind off your hardship are legion when you allow them. And they increase the more you allow them. It is possible for us to choose what we train our consciousness on, but most of us operate in stimulus/react autopilot that keeps us uneasy or unhappy if not miserable. We are rarely if ever in control of our circumstances, but we can always be in control of what we make of them. Usually, if we think we are in control, it is just an illusion. We can choose to be happy or at least peaceful. My life would have been easier if I was shown this at an early age. Thank God, I know it now. I do not think I could make a trip like this at this age without this knowledge—and certainly not think it was fun.

When we start to become more self-aware, we see how much we bolster one another's negativity. It is a perfectly normal part of our communal existence. I noticed when I would bemoan a situation to a friend or relative and expand on my sad story, they would usually offer, "You have the right to feel that way." This is what passes for support among us.

It is normal, but it is egregiously incorrect. Our mental health as individuals and as a species would improve immensely if we were taught that our minds are generally not good arbiters of our equanimity. It is easy to see in blatant bouts of insanity such as mass murders, school shootings, and any act of vengeance. But these stem from subtle underpinnings in our everyday lives that are equivalent to mass lunacy.

"My wife left me; she is a bitch."

"My husband left me; I am not good enough."

"The person in front of me is driving too slow. Asshole."

"I can't afford enough makeup to fit in; I'm a loser."

"I don't have the right tennis shoes. No respect."

"My lawn has weeds; what will people think?"

"This bicycle in the road is slowing me down. They shouldn't be allowed on the highway."

He should; they should; she should; we should; it should; I should; you should.

Should is the unhappiest word in English. It immediately connotes a state of dissatisfaction, and the utterer almost always has a sense of righteousness.

When this first became evident to me, I would catch myself. After uttering or even thinking a few "shoulds," I would tell myself that I had just should all over myself. Every time we pass judgement on someone else, we are conveniently overlooking an important part of ourselves. This is a damaging, unnecessary habit. It is normal and very difficult to break at first. With practice it is glaringly obvious.

Had I known what I was going to end up doing today, I could have saved myself a lot of miles when I came to Highway 257. It is a terrific shortcut to get over to Highways 20/26, on which I would leave Casper eventually. But I was cold and hungry and wanted coffee. I couldn't wait to get out of the weather for a bit. I didn't see any mom-and-pop restaurants, but I did see a QDOBA with a Starbucks next door. I had never been in a QDOBA before, and I was delighted to find a menu full of healthy choices. My wife, the healthy eater, would be happy here. I had an excellent meal and then planted myself next door in Starbucks. It was too early to get a motel room, so I looked over my choices and the route ahead. It was about 100 miles to Shoshoni on 20/26, and there was not going to be much in the way of services. I looked at the specifics that I could find for Natrona, Waltman, Hiland, and Moneta. It seemed possible that I would not find any services the entire way. Then came a game-changing observation. I looked at the Windy.com app, and my heartfelt resolve to get a motel room vanished.

I was sitting there in Starbucks with the wind blowing 24 MPH out of the east. I would have a powerful tailwind if I left right then. I looked at the Windy prediction for the next day, and it said 14 MPH westerly. The day after was calling for the same. In fact, there was no easterly predicted for the rest of the week. So, the choice was cozy up in a cherished motel room now and leave Casper during headwinds or leave right now in the glory of a 24-MPH tail windstorm.

I guess that really wasn't a choice. I packed up and rushed out the door.

It took a bit to wend my way out of Casper with one stop to pick up a canned coffee drink for the morning. Then I blazed. I had never had that strong of a tailwind before. It was sublime. As hard as I could pedal, I could still feel the wind pushing on my back. The road was very good. Rumble strips came and went, but there was always plenty of shoulder beside them.

There was a lot of traffic considering that I was heading deeper into nowhere. I'm not sure where they were all going, but the whole time I rode, there were cars. Perhaps because this was one of the ways to either the south or east entrances to Yellowstone.

I came to Natrona, and there was nothing. Nothing! Just a bare intersection. Powder River was just a small collection of houses. I raced on. Waltman was an even smaller collection of houses. I was glad that I was well provisioned. The wind seemed to be gusting higher now, and I blithely pedaled on, blissfully unaware that there was a rainstorm overtaking me.

When big drops started to fall, I pulled over into a very wide spot in the road. I was ill-prepared for this and had to dig my rain gear and shoe covers out of my left rear pannier. The shoe covers were deep down in. This would be my first time wearing them.

My rain gear is super light and super cheap. It is also very baggy and bright yellow. It is one thing to be visible in the flow of traffic, but cars approaching from a side road do not have wipers on their side windows, and their vision is obscured by raindrops. The baggy bright yellow is paramount. To me it is better to be visible rather than sporty-looking.

I sat on the wet pavement to put on my rain pants and shoe covers. There is no choice for me. With my gimpiness I can no more step into shoes or pants than fly to the moon. I sat on my raincoat too, but everything was wet the minute it came out of the packs. The wind was so strong that Truckee kept blowing over on me, and I had to catch it several times. It was like a circus act—clown division. I scooched up to pull my rain pants up, and my rain jacket took off flying across the road. When I got my baggy pants up, I was ready to chase down my rain jacket and hoped on Truckee. The leg of my rain pants immediately got blown into the front sprocket and caught in the chain. As I mentioned, my rain outfit was super light and super cheap, so I was able to just get a handful of pant leg and jerk it out of the bind.

I tore the pant leg the rest of the way through the cuff and then tied it shut. The cinching was enough to keep it from getting caught in the chain again. Now I gave chase for my raincoat.

Luckily, it had kited down into an opening in the brush, and I was able to retrieve it without much trouble. Once I got it on and was back on the road, I found myself in an enviable position. The weather was cool enough that I was not hot pedaling like hell in my rain gear. The rain outfit was billowy enough that it helped like a sail. I made incredible mileage.

Hiland went by in the failing light. It looked like there might have been a gas station there. (As I am writing this, I have noticed that between Hiland and Moneta is the exact center of the state of Wyoming.)

Darkness fell, the rain moved on, and I kept going. Since I was traveling alone, I could be an idiot if I wanted. Once before, on my first trip, I stopped for the night in a stiff tailwind. I even had a difficult time setting up my flopping tent. The next morning, I awoke with the wind blowing in the opposite direction. I was not going to let that happen again.

I did not put my lights on because I didn't want to waste time stopping in that wind. There are huge reflective patches on the backs of my panniers, so I knew the drivers could see me from far away. I could hear them changing lanes to stay clear of me. The shoulder was wide enough that I could stay well out of the traffic anyway. Of course, all this is relative. Non-cyclers (and intelligent people) would have probably felt unsafe.

The wind was letting up, and I was extremely tired. I passed Moneta, and there was nothing there. I think the town was off the main road somewhere.

The wind died completely, and my frenetic pace dissipated. I was slowly pedaling along looking for a camping spot in the dark. Stealth did not matter. This is all BLM land with a barbed-wire fence that travels alongside the road about 100 feet from it. Now and again, there would be a gate in the fence where a small access road would pass through. I planned on camping at one of these gates, but none were forthcoming. I was completely fatigued from an incredible day of exertion—played out. I had completely overdone it.

At one point I fell partially in the road. (Remember, I said idiot.) I scrambled to get out from under the bike, and then I walked the bike. I was too tired to ride and too tired to walk, but there was no side road—no camping spot.

I walked Truckee a very long way before a police vehicle pulled up behind me with his flashing lights on. He was from the town of Shoshoni. He said that a motorist called in about a cyclist on the side of the road. I told him that yes, I fell and now I was walking to look for a camp spot. He offered to give me a ride to Shoshoni and said his wife could come out and get the bike with their pickup truck. Such nice people.

I thanked him and said I would prefer just to camp around here for the night. He called the state troopers and asked if I was allowed to camp up by the barbed-wire fence even though it was technically the right-of-way. They said fine. He used his bright flashlights to help me get over to the fence to set up. When I finally got into my sleeping bag, it was 11:50 p.m. The windstorm and my folly had pushed me to a new all-time mileage record despite my long pause in Casper.

108 miles.

CHAPTER 13

Wind River

I slept in a little the next morning and felt very fresh when I got up. The sun was up in a mostly cloudy sky—an excellent start. The temperature was in the mid-40s. That strong easterly had steered warmer weather my way. And thanks to my marathon yesterday, I was in range of a restaurant breakfast, or so I thought.

I got back on the road, and within 300 yards, I came upon an access road of the type I was looking for last night. One that would usher me to the barbed-wire fence gate for a decent campsite. Oh well, I had no qualms with last night's experience.

I rode past a saloon, so I thought the odds were decent for finding a sit-down breakfast. It is always nice to find somewhere to sit down that isn't a bicycle seat. Right at the intersection where 20 turns north, I stopped at the Exxon Food Mart. I asked inside if there was a sit-down restaurant around. The very friendly guy behind the counter said no. If I wanted some food at this hour, this was it. He said the saloon would be open later.

It was as big as convenience stores come in the desert, and they had a lot of grab-and-go type of prepared food. It was not the horrible stuff you get in a lot of smaller places. And they actually had good coffee with real half-and-half creamer. One of the coffee canisters was labeled "organic." I had not seen that label on anything for quite some time. I grabbed a breakfast burrito and sat with my coffee at one of the inside benches. Heaven!

I surveyed my map, and some people came over and asked all the usual questions. When they left, I grabbed another breakfast burrito. It was only 32 miles to Thermopolis, but ya never know. I topped off my water bottles in case of unexpected delays. I figured if all went well, I could get there in time for a late lunch and get a room somewhere that offered a thermal pool. Might as well luxuriate if the option materialized.

The Boysen Reservoir is a huge lake lying out in the middle of the desert. I could see it off to my left as I traversed more vastness. I had been sending pictures to a California friend who commented that all my pictures were of enormous expansiveness. Such is the grandness of the western states. This area would be utterly unlivable if not for the Wind River. I was 16 miles from the start of the Wind River Canyon. I had no idea what to expect. I knew I was going to be following down the Wind River as it wound through the canyon it had carved over the ages. It was 16 miles of barren land. There was habitation along a little bit of the lake shore—businesses that were dependent on recreation customers.

I entered the canyon from the south. The first thing I came to were three tunnels. There was not enough room for the road and the railroad track to share the thin cut in the escarpment where the river flows north. After that, I was treated to 17 of the best miles I have ever ridden on a bicycle. The road was very good, and the amount of room available for a bicycle was everywhere between excellent and uh-oh. I was glad to be going downhill though there were places it looked like the river was flowing uphill. It is an optical illusion that has been talked about since humans. The early Native Americans said that there were two rivers in the canyon. One flowing in each direction.

The road stays on the east side of the canyon and the railroad on the west side. Someone bent a lot of steel to lay those tracks. The walls of the canyon are over 2000 feet high, and the canyon is known for its wind hazards.

Wind hazards in a vehicle are one thing, but on a bicycle they are far more dangerous. Today, the wind was blowing about 16 MPH from behind me as had been my luck recently. There were several hair-raising spots where the canyon squeezed the roadway for which shoulder width was forfeited. There the wind was likewise funneled, upping the chance for dangerous wind shear. I didn't mind keeping my hands on the brakes because I was certainly in no hurry to end this extraordinary ride. The fortuity of getting to bicycle through this majestic topography was never once lost on me. Did I mention I was lucky?

Upon exiting the canyon, things really changed. When I entered the canyon, it was the Wind River, but now it was the Bighorn River. It would be my companion for a few days. I would follow it to the town of Greybull.

It is much greener on this side due to all the irrigation. I squeezed out of that narrow gorge back into open country. Beautiful but without the grandeur of the Wind River Canyon.

Thermopolis had all the services you could want. It survives mainly on tourism, but it has a nice, quaint feel to it. I made a reservation at the Days Inn. They had a spa pool and a restaurant, so I would not have to get on my bike again once I arrived. Though I arrived too early to check in, they let me use the spa pool while they readied the room. There was a nice dressing room with showers, so I didn't need the room right away anyway. The spa pool had natural, geothermally heated mineral water with only a hint of sulfur smell. As you might imagine, it was an awesome break after all that riding.

This was Day 53. I tried to think when my last motel night was. It was the night of Day 49 in Laramie. When was my last machine laundry? Hmmm—Day 47 before I left Tom and Becky's in Denver. I was going to do machine laundry here, so it felt like it was getting regular. Normally, every motel night is laundry hand-wash night. When I leave a motel, all my riding ensembles start out clean. This place happened to have a coin-op guest laundry, so I could wash my jackets too. I had a puffy, packable jacket that was usually too warm to ride in, but not lately. I had a thin, bright green jacket that I wore over it for visibility. Some of these cold nights, I slept in both to make up for the thin spots in my down bag, and I almost always slept in my bright yellow beanie hat. I also wore the beanie on the road to keep my ears warm. All of it gets washed on a laundromat night. Gloves too.

When it is below 40 degrees with wind, riding without some kind of gloves is way less fun. By this point I was on my third pair of gloves as I managed to lose one or the other along the way and must replace them. I do not travel in expensive biking gloves. I started out with yellow, $7 Walmart gloves that I really liked. One cannot always wait for a Walmart to show up. The pair I have now I bought at the farm store in Sheridan Lake, Colorado.

When my room was ready, I jumped out of the spa pool and unloaded my bike in the room. I padded down the hall and put my laundry in a machine. What a luxury!

This hotel had been some kind of hunter's club, and there were mounted animal heads all over the place. When I was a youngster, my cousin and I would dream of traveling the world killing different things—one of everything if possible. We were brought up to believe that hunting animals had some kind of nobility attached to it. Both of us outgrew that, but from the Days Inn decor, it looks like many people hadn't. Such is the world. I marvel at the way our lives' paths meander.

However, meandering might be a kind interpretation. A case could be made for us being dragged around by our nostrils as if there were rings in them. We develop egos early and are taught to give service to them without questioning how we got such ruinous ideas. We take these ideas for granted until something gets us to look at them. Then the difference between reality and what we make of it is glaring. For a lot of people, this realization never happens. Some never find out that life is so much better than our habits.

After dinner, I went back out to the spa pool. There were six people in it now. It was fun. There was a couple from Montana who made regular forays down to Thermopolis. There was another couple that, like me, were there for the first time. The third couple was from West Palm Beach, Florida. Of course, I had to ask if they knew my pals who lived in West Palm. As if it was a little burg. I used to get that a lot when I worked in Alaska. I would be "outside," which was an Alaskan term for anywhere but Alaska. People would hear I was from up there and would ask if I knew so-and-so. Never did I, but I would guess the odds were better that I knew their acquaintance than these people from West Palm knowing my friends.

Once I was in Guangzhou, China, speaking to a local who said he had a friend from Alaska in town. He arranged for us to meet, and it turned out that the guy worked in the fishing industry out of Kodiak, which was where I worked. The friend and I knew a lot of people in common, but we had never heard of each other. Pretty cool.

After the spa festivities, I went back to my room and packed all my clean laundry. I planned to go to the house breakfast when it opened in the morning and eat everything I could stuff in. This break was fun, but it was enough. I was ready to hit the road.

42 miles.

There was still a slight, southerly wind, so the morning ride started well. On the way out of town, I stopped at some overlooks for viewing the giant hot spring. They claimed it to be the world's largest mineral hot spring. I can't guess how these things might be measured and compared. I've seen Mammoth Hot Springs in Yellowstone, and it is certainly large. There, they claimed to have the "largest carbonate-depositing spring" in the world. They are both worth seeing… amazing phenomena.

I rode north as the wind picked up and took a more westerly tack. Lucerne, Kirby, Winchester. I was determined to ride to Worland before stopping.

In Worland I stopped at the Cenex gas station/convenience store. I had a choice. Stay on Highway 20, crossing the Bighorn River, and traveling through town up the east side of the river was one. The other choice was to avoid town altogether and turn north on Highway 433 on the west side of the river. Either way, both routes met again in Manderson about 21 miles away.

Of course, I have no idea what the eastern side looked like, but I chose the road on the western side, which rose high above the river and passed through very beautiful farmland. The Bighorn Canal was on my side all the way to the turnoff just before Manderson. I did not cross the Bighorn River again. Highway 20 came across and met me, and we went up to Basin, Wyoming.

I wasn't expecting the town of Basin to be as large as it was. It seemed to have everything a cyclist could need. I was hot, so I stopped in Wheeler's Basin's Market for an ice cream. I never eat ice cream at home in Florida, but on a trip like this, calories and carbohydrates disappear like magic. I aimed to keep going and spend the night in Greybull.

When I arrived in Greybull, I started actively looking for an actual campsite. I guess I had forgotten why I normally eschew campgrounds, public or private. I pulled into a lovely, small, private campground and went in the office. A perfectly wonderful lady told me that they charged $25 for a tent site. I was hoping for $10 per night. (My wife is fond of telling me how far behind the times I am.) Before I could respond, the lady commented on what tent camping had done to her lawn. I could tell that she did not care if I stayed there, and luckily, neither did I. She said that there was a rest area west of town and that I might look at that. I bid her best wishes and headed out of town to the west.

The thing about people giving a cyclist directions is that neither usually understands what each is saying. Not very far for a vehicle driver can be a very long way on a bicycle. And the cyclist, especially one who has ridden all day, can feel like a distance is even farther. It reminds me of the guy back in Eads, Colorado who told me that Highway 86 was hilly. I found that highway to be the hill grind from hell. Perhaps that was what he had been trying to tell me.

I crossed a creek and the railroad tracks in an annoying high wind. I guessed that the wind speed had come up to the low 20s. Setting up my tent was going to be tedious. There was a righthand turn up ahead with some buildings on the right. It looked like a fairground, but there was nothing labeling it. The gate was open. To a stealth camper, an open gate without a "no trespassing" indication equals a welcome sign.

I immediately came upon a very small wooden shed with a tin roof. It had a gravel floor and was big enough to accommodate both my bedroll and Truckee—but just. I was thankful to be out of that wind. I had no more set up my bed on the floor when a pickup truck pulling a large horse trailer drove into the fairground area and parked just past my hideout.

I will never know if they saw me or not… but one of their horses surely did. It was quite late in the day as they drove past my shed, and they would have been blind not to see me as they drove past the open door. They unloaded five horses but left one tied to the trailer. They were gone riding for nearly an hour, and the entire time the horse that was left tied to the trailer stared at my shed. It was funny to see how concerned, but not unduly, the horse was about my occupancy. Every time I looked out through the cracks in the shed, the horse was looking at me.

Just before dark, they loaded up all their horses and left. I remained in the peace of that shed with the wind howling outside. I thank those equestrians.

70 miles.

I left my shed in Greybull at first morning light. I rode back into town and had an excellent breakfast and coffee at Bob's Diner. It was a family-run diner and had a family feel to it. The people were awesome.

When I left Greybull, the wind traveled with me and then against me. Never all that powerfully. I stayed on US Highway 310 through Lovell, then Cowley. In Cowley I had a nice lunch at the Bull Pub. I wondered what a pub like this was like for locals. I was a stranger stopping at an off hour. It was quiet for my visit.

The seven miles from Cowley to Deaver sucked. The entire distance the pavement was grooved for resurfacing. I had to concentrate on the constant changes in the road surface. Even more than the constant watching for glass, screws, rocks, nails, wire, and other unidentified poking objects that was normal.

I passed through Deaver without slowing down and continued to Frannie, the last town in Wyoming. I was hoping for some services in Frannie, but they were slight. There was a Wyoming Port of Entry station that looked closed and little else. Thankfully, as I was leaving town, I came to a little saloon on the left side of the road. I was only two miles from Montana, but I knew there was not going to be anything for a very long way.

There were a couple of ladies sitting at the bar and a woman bartender. I was an anomaly there to say the least. It was fun to talk to them about my adventure and to hear about life in Frannie, Wyoming. They were happy to warn me that there was nothing on the other side of the border until Bridger, Montana 28 miles away. I bought a couple of bottles of beer for my quiet celebration upon reaching Montana and left.

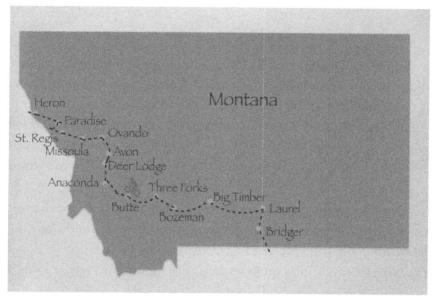

The Frannie Canal and I crossed into Montana close together. As promised, there was nothing at the border except a welcome sign. I took some selfies there and rolled on. The terrain was an amazingly vast area of nothingness. It was beautiful in a disquieting way. This part of Montana did not have the wide road shoulder that I had enjoyed in Wyoming, but then, vehicles were a rarity.

I traveled about 10 miles into Montana and then set my tent up close to the road. There was so little traffic that, again, I didn't care. I cared more that there was no telephone reception. I could not check my wind or weather apps. There wasn't any choice anyway. I had one road to travel and one direction.

I reflected on the luck I had in choosing this way across Wyoming and into Montana. I did not get to bike through Yellowstone Park, but I was privileged to see a lot of great expanses that I otherwise would not have. This wide valley with snowcapped mountain ranges far to the east and west was one of them.

65 miles.

In a prescient safeguard I had put up my rainfly last night. Since I didn't have reception to check for rain, I put it up as a precaution. The ground outside was dry and cracked when I went to bed.

It rained and blew overnight. I woke up at five thirty very relaxed and thankful to be dry. I was surprised to see that the ground was still dry and cracked when I got up. I guess it takes a lot of rain to moisten all that dry.

Once I got on my bike, I found myself treated to a delicious downhill coast for nine miles. It could have been 11 miles, but the wind suddenly came up hard against me, and I had to pedal down the last two miles. It is quite an exquisite bummer to have to pedal downhill against the wind. Every XC cyclist has encountered this. The wind was slightly against me the rest of the day. Those legendary tailwinds had ended again.

I pushed against a mild wind to Rockvale. I just wanted a snack and to keep going. I stopped at the Rockvale Travel Plaza, grabbed a bite, and moved on. Oddly, there were slot machines inside. I would eventually find out that gambling machines were in every convenience store, gas station, and nook and cranny in Montana. There were lots of casinos in the bigger towns and seemingly at every place where two major highways intersected.

GMB showed me the option of taking the road less traveled, Clarks River Road. I took it. It was nice to get away from the busy highway I had gotten on that led into Rockvale. I encountered some unwelcome spitting rain before I met up with US Highway 310/212 just outside of Laurel. You don't know these things when traveling by bicycle, so I was surprised to see a huge petrochemical plant and a giant rail yard in Laurel. I wanted to keep going, but there were also massive, dark clouds threatening in the westerly direction, so I took a room at the Locomotive Inn.

I biked over to the Walmart in town. One of the things l like about Walmart is they always let me bring my bike inside. At this Walmart the lady inside the door asked me where I had biked from. When I told her Florida, she was excited. Her enthusiasm was delightful. She called another fellow over, and they both congratulated me on such an accomplishment. She had to borrow a phone so she could get a selfie with me. We all took photos and they told me that I was inspiring. That was a fun stop. I returned to the Locomotive Inn and planned some of the next day's route.

52 miles.

Only two nights on the road between motel rooms. I felt like I was spoiling myself. On my GoFundMe I had asked for a little extra funding for weather-dodging accommodation. Last night certainly qualified. I could not hear the rain during the night, but everything was soaking wet in the morning, and there were puddles everywhere. The sky was completely overcast with dark, lumpy clouds, but the weather app said go. There was a slight chance of pockets of rain.

I was at the hotel breakfast as soon as it was set up, and I pounded down food and coffee as usual. GMB suggested I leave town on "Old Highway 10."

US Highway 10 would have been the old way of crossing southern Montana, but after Interstate 90 was put through, there were just remnants of the old 10. Most of what is left is a cyclist's dream. Highway 10 is like a frontage road for Interstate 90, but better. In many places it wanders far from the Interstate through lovely landscapes. I feel a little sorry for people traveling by Interstate Highway. They are missing something... everything.

I started today on the north side of I-90 and traveled through flat land. But I also started out dragging. I'm not sure why. Some days are like that. It takes eight or 10 miles to get over the lag. I hadn't had a morning like this in a while.

In Park City I crossed under the Interstate and came upon a large Cenex gas station. The convenience store was spacious with inside seating. I grabbed a coffee and sat down at a table. I thought that sitting around for a little while might be the ticket to get energized again.

A woman came over and asked me if that was my bicycle outside. She asked me about my trip and how it was going and offered to buy me breakfast. I thanked her and said I had a huge breakfast back in Laurel. She knew the ropes because she had done some XC cycling in her 20s. She spent weeks riding up through Canada and said that people were extremely helpful. I told her that I was having a similar experience. She added that she was in a good place in her life now and wanted to help me. She handed me $20 and left.

Good karma shining through! People were good to her in the past, and she wanted to pass that goodness along. I'm sure she has suffered some hardships in her past brought on by others, but she did not choose to carry that forward. This is always the choice. Always! One person chooses to focus on their woes, and one person chooses to focus on their joy. Whose life is better? Who do you think has more energy, more verve? Which one brings on a better world? It is not the situation that guides this. It never is. It is the understanding with which we respond to the situation.

After that encounter I was inspired to get back out on Old US 10. Interstate 90, Old Highway 10 and I were traveling alongside the Yellowstone River. I was going upstream. 10 stayed closer to the river and it was beautiful riding. There was a railroad track between me and the river. I found myself wondering if the railroad engineers ever got tired of traveling through the stunning scenery.

Highway 10 had many hills on it that the Interstate would have lacked. But at the tops of these hills, there were always postcard-worthy scenes of the river and the snowcapped mountains to the south that delineated the Yellowstone Caldera. I felt privileged again at getting to ride this route.

Eventually, though, I had to get on the Interstate where Old 10 was giving up for a while. I crossed the river on I-90 and got off on a frontage road. The frontage road turned back into my friend Old 10. I was on the other (southern) side of the river, but it was just as beautiful. The Interstate stayed to the south of me so as not to impair my river view.

After Greycliff, Old 10 and the Interstate swapped places up to Big Timber. I topped off my water in Big Timber and started keeping an eye out for a stealth camp site.

I got all the way to Springdale without finding a suitable site. Springdale itself was just a collection of houses. I saw on GMB that there was a fishing access at the river. I rolled down there and found the most beautiful spot of all my camps. There was a little park with a few picnic tables and a pit toilet. This find was slightly marred by a "No Camping" sign. Nevertheless, I had ridden over 80 miles and simply couldn't look further. I put my tent up on the riverbank behind some bushes. It would serve as stealth for this occasion. It was too-good-to-be-true gorgeous. I was sure that no one in Yellowstone Park had a better campsite on the river. As usual, I hoped that I wasn't spotted by anyone who really cared. Two people walked down to the river from Springdale and we exchanged glances, and I guess they didn't care. I had an exquisite night there. I couldn't believe my luck. Such beauty. Natural serenity as good as it gets. Peace profound.

85 miles.

I hated to leave this site, but ride I must. Just upstream from my stealth camp was a cement bridge that crossed over the river. The road was called Convict Grade Road. The bridge supported an inundation of swallows. There were so many that they were noisy. I stopped on the bridge to watch them. The flock churned below the bridge. All of them in a hurry, none of them going anywhere. It reminded me of the human predicament.

GMB said that Convict Grade Road was a back-road choice for getting to Livingston, my next large town. It was very tempting, but I could see it was going to turn into a dirt road, and there was always the chance it would get worse.

A car came from the direction I wanted to go, and I flagged it down. The lone woman was charming. I asked her how the road was from there to Livingston. She said that it was pretty good and that she rode her mountain bike on it all the time. She also warned me that Livingston was an expensive place. She said that lots of famous people live in the area.

It was very tempting to take Convict Grade Road since there was a hefty headwind, and I would not make good time anyway. But pretty good on a mountain bike could easily turn into hell on Truckee. I decided to turn around and get back on the frontage road.

I had to ride on the Interstate for a few miles before I could pick back up on the frontage road. The wind was blowing hard out of the west, and I was struggling. I had to remind myself of tailwinds I had known, and that I had to pay up somewhere. I was paying now… big time.

I encountered a warning sign that said, "Gusty Winds Area." There was a windsock on top of the sign that was blowing straight out toward the direction I had come. I would not get to Livingston soon enough.

Eventually, I was charmed by Livingston and not just because of the time-out from the war with the headwind. The downtown area was filled with old buildings that gave it such character. Livingston was an offspring of the Northern Pacific Railway. In the middle 1800s the railroad needed a spot to service steam engines before they went over Bozeman Pass to the west. It was the highest pass on their route across the country. There is still a lot of railroad activity in town. Several times I saw engines with no cars coming from the west. It looked like they hitched engines to the rear of westbound trains to help push them over the pass.

The city is also known as the gateway to Yellowstone National Park. Gardiner, Yellowstone's north entrance, is 50 very scenic miles south of Livingston.

I spent the whole day in town because the wind was just too much to fight against. I used up too much water grinding against the wind. I rode around town a bit and had a nap in a park. The blow was unrelenting. I decided to ease out of town on… Old Highway 10… because I eventually needed to find a campsite.

I had to pedal hard going downhill out of town. I stopped at the Yellowstone Truck Stop for a meal. The place was packed, and there was only one waitress. I was finding situations like this all across America. Something about COVID had caused this effect. There were "help wanted" signs everywhere across the country. There might have been only one person in the kitchen at this place also. The food took a long time, and it wasn't as good as one could hope.

When I left the truck stop, darkness was falling. I had to set up camp—soon. I knew I was going to have to settle on a site of poor quality, so it helped that it would be dark right away.

I came upon the open gate to a yard that had to be active during the day. There was farm equipment around and a row of large round hay bales. If I used this as a stealth camp, I would have to leave it early in the morning. The countryside was expansive and spare. You could see for miles. That was one of the beauties of the Livingston area. But it did not lend itself to stealth camping. There were no woods to hide in.

I erected my tent against the row of hay bales on the side opposite the road. Not that it mattered. Traffic numbers had fallen to zero. It was a comfortable spot for sleeping. The ground was covered with flattened grass. I got cozied in and set my alarm for 5 a.m. I read for a bit as the teeny nap today interfered with going right to sleep. It was still windy, so my tent was flapping. The wind was supposed to be against me tomorrow again, but only three to five MPH.

29 miles.

The temperature was 34 degrees at five in the morning. When I broke camp and hit the road, the wind was six MPH straight in my face. It was still dark. Biking conditions were less than ideal to say the least. At this point my odyssey lacked glamor. Hmmm, did it ever have any? Well, yes… just the night before camping along the Yellowstone River!

It took me two hours to go 10 miles, including conquering Bozeman Pass. Once over the pass, the wind had died out, and the going was better getting into Bozeman, Montana. GMB wanted me to get to Bozeman by a back way, but I elected not trust it. I didn't want to get back up in the hills and then have the road turn into a mountain biking trail.

I had been riding for hours, but with such an early start, I was in Bozeman in time for breakfast. This was another very charming town with lots of old buildings and majestic mountains all around. It is the home of Montana State University, which explained the presence of many youthful people. I asked a young couple for a breakfast recommendation, and they did not hesitate to suggest the Western Café.

The café was very busy, and I had to wait for a seat at the counter. The recommendation was solid. Though it was busy, the service was fast, and my breakfast was excellent. I left there and continued down Main Street. I liked Bozeman, but I kept rolling. The continental divide was coming up, and I wanted to get that behind me. I had been thinking about it since Florida. I could have crossed the divide back in Colorado, but it would have taken going over some 10- or 12,000-foot pass. I was looking to cross at a lower elevation. The lowest place to cross the divide was on Interstate 90 between Bozeman and Butte. That was the Homestake Pass at 6,375 feet. I had already been over a higher elevation than that all the way back in Laramie, Wyoming. But since then, I had lost considerable elevation. Bozeman was only 4,810 feet; I was still losing elevation as I headed toward the divide. I would drop all the way down to 4,075 feet at Three Forks, which meant the approach to the pass was going to be short and steep.

I stopped at Starbucks on my way out of town and had coffee at an outside table. The weather had turned terrific. Ian stopped and introduced himself to me. He was a software engineer who was also an avid hiker. He knew the area well. I was able to ask him about my other option for going over the continental divide. There was the small Highway 2 that went over Pipestone Pass. It was less than 100 feet higher than Homestake Pass. He said the road was narrow and winding, and the shoulder came and went. He told me Homestake Pass on I-90 was one long, steep up—then some down and then a short, steep up.

We sat around leisurely enjoying the coffee, conversation, and excellent weather.

The option of taking Highway 2 was not a good one for me. It takes me a long time to negotiate hills, especially if I have to get off and push. With little or no road shoulder, it would be far more dangerous for me and for drivers trying to avoid me. On the Interstate I have my own wide lane (most of the time), and I can get off my bike as much as needed without being in the roadway. Pedal on...

At Three Forks several streams come together to start the headwaters of the Missouri River. It was funny to wade into a creek that would become such a mighty river. Some of this water would flow past New Orleans and into the Gulf of Mexico. Imagine!

I topped off my water because I wasn't sure what was ahead of me. I was going to travel some back roads before reconnecting with Interstate 90 for crossing Homestake Pass.

GMB had recommended leaving Three Forks via the Old Yellowstone Trail. I was nervous about riding on a road named Trail because of the likelihood of it turning to dirt. But I knew it was going to connect to US 287 and then Highway 2.

My cautionary instincts served me. There was almost no traffic on this straight road, and I ended up in a town called Willow Creek. It was a nice little agricultural town that even had a café/saloon. To connect with 287, I was going to have to get on Meridian Cemetery Road, which, of course, was dirt.

I had the option to ride all the way back to Three Forks to cut over to a paved road, but that was a seven-mile backtrack. Truckee and I eschew backtracking. Well... I don't think Truckee cares.

I thought I'd try the dirt road for a bit, and if it didn't look like it was going to work out, I could backtrack. Besides, it was getting close to stealth camp time. This dirt road might present a good opportunity.

The dirt was firm and not rocky or gravelly. The Jefferson River drained the area, and I don't think it had rained in a while. There was a decent chance that it wouldn't turn muddy on me. I did see some pretty good stealth camping opportunities, but it was still a bit early.

The route led across the Jefferson River on what looked like an old rail bridge. The sturdy bridge seemed out of place for this dirt road. Eventually, I made it out to 287. Not a bad shortcut at all. But then I had to find a camp spot, and I was running out of steam. The countryside continued to be wide open without any place to hide. I had to do a roadside camp.

287 was a series of hills. I stopped Truckee at the top of one of them and pushed it through the weeds to the fence. I had to be careful of several small cacti both walking the bike and laying out my ground tarp.

I liked the spot because from the top of this rise I could see across the Jefferson River Valley. It looked like I could see all the way back to Three Forks. I was less than 100 feet off the road, but there were only a few cars passing before dark and none afterward.

I have had several unfortunate encounters with cactus. Into every life a little cactus thorn must fall. The normal reaction is to just pull away. We humans often behave like stimulus-reaction machines. It is easy to see that with a cactus thorn, or a hot stove, or ice-cold water. Easy! But what about the endless stimuli that we react to with our minds or with our hearts? And why do different people react differently to the same stimulus? In the answer to those two questions lies the crux of why we—you and I—everyone is either happy or unhappy. It is why we are experiencing either equanimity or agitation. It is why there is war or there is peace. We all could do with more equanimity.

CHAPTER 14

Chasing Equanimity

We assume our problems lie outside of ourselves because we are taught that the problems lie outside of ourselves. That is simply not true. Situations lie outside of us, but we make them into problems.

A long time ago, I was talking to Toby, my motorcycle friend, about some dumb thing that someone did driving in front of me. It was minor, but he could see I was still agitated over it. He said that he never gets upset about what other drivers do around him.

Of course, that was not the response I expected, wanted, or hoped for. He was supposed to do what is normal—what our friends are meant to do. He was supposed to chime in with something like, "Yeah, what an asshole," or "Yeah, you have the right to feel that way."

His actual response defused me. My ego-bomb wanted to blow up, but it was literally defused. I had the option to go away and find someone to side with me to keep the fuse lit, or I could instead see myself. I could stop and see that my reaction was totally within me. Toby would have a different reaction in that situation and not be upset.

This can be applied to any and every situation that befalls us. All we need to do is see when we are upset, hurt, angry, or anxious. No matter how hard we are pushed to think the feelings are useful, they are not warranted and do not help. With some skillful self-examination, we can see how we are either contributing to equanimity or contributing to anxiety. Once we see this, we don't need to do anything. We will change quickly without effort.

The night was clear, and I could feel that it was going to be cold.
 71 miles.

I stayed in bed a little longer than I might have. It was 30 degrees when I woke up. I was about seven miles from the Lewis and Clark Caverns State Park, and I was hoping I could find some hot coffee there. It was a quick and cold ride down to the Jefferson River basin. I was traveling through a lovely, wide canyon against the current of the Jefferson River.

Within a few miles, I was quite surprised to come upon a giant, vacant festival area. There was a line-up of rows and rows of pit toilets, and an enormous car park and camping area. It turns out that every year, they hold the "Rockin' the Rivers" rock festival there for three days. And at some short time before or after, they have the Headwaters Country Jam music festival that also lasts three days. With no one around, it would have been a terrific spot for my stealth camp had I continued a little further last night.

I rode on to the Lewis and Clark Caverns State Park. Thankfully, the visitor's center was down at the lower elevation. It was a lovely place, very well maintained. I looked around at the presentations inside. I did not know that it was the largest limestone cave in the Northwest. It turns out that Lewis and Clark never knew of its existence though their party camped along the Jefferson River below it.

The visitor's center did not have coffee on offer, and the actual cave was 1000 feet higher up on a good bikeable trail. I would like to have gone up there, but physically, I just couldn't. I had passed a billboard a while back that said there was breakfast, lunch, and dinner four miles past the park, so I rode on to LaHood through a beautiful area where the river basin narrowed spectacularly. Again came the feeling of privilege at getting to see such an area by bicycle.

I must admit to some disappointment when I arrived in LaHood. One side of the road featured a couple of abandoned-looking buildings, the other a nice building that was now labeled the LaHood Park Steakhouse. It was closed. It had some nice benches outside that were in the shade, so I relaxed with a snack. I was thinking about the billboard that I saw miles ago when a guy came out of the building. He told me it was a steakhouse now that would open at three. I mentioned the breakfast, lunch, and dinner billboard, and he said that sign was more than 10 years old. Hmmm.

There was no sense arguing with reality… there never is. I could easily slay any equanimity with a tirade of remarks. "Why don't they take the sign down?" "Who is in charge of these things?" "What am I supposed to do now?"

The exquisite, beautiful realization is that we are going to go on to do whatever is next regardless of all the negativity slinging. We will certainly be better within, as will anyone we encounter, if we let the negative stuff go. We have the power.

There was a gas station two miles away and the town of Whitehall eight miles after that. (I found out since I finished my trip that the steakhouse burned to the ground several months later.)

The next thing I came to was the Cardwell Store and RV Park and the Moose Crossing Sweets and Gifts. I wasn't sure where one started and the other left off, but the guys inside were happy to let me fill my water bottles. I asked about coffee and was told they had Americanos next door. There was a young fellow acting as barista who told me they also had quality ice cream. Well… one vice at a time. I chose the Americano.

Sitting outside at a picnic table, a semitruck driver joined me for a bit. He talked about driving around there forever and all the changes. I asked him if I could buy him a coffee, but he was set. He reiterated that the climb up Homestake Pass was steep.

When I left there, I crossed under the Interstate and got on MT-69 that took me into Whitehall. I did not stop. I was on a mission now—get over the Homestake Pass. I was coffeed up, and a six MPH easterly wind was ready to help me as much as it could.

GMB showed me that I could stay off the Interstate for a little longer. After that, Interstate 90 would be the friend to help me get over the continental divide.

When I got back onto I-90, I was 25 miles past Whitehall. Whitehall sat at elevation 4,360, and I had not gained much elevation since then. Maybe a few hundred feet. I was now approximately 13 miles from the top of Homestake Pass and had to gain about 1,800 feet in elevation. Let's not forget how old and gimpy a fella we are talking about here. It was exhausting just thinking about it... but here is the thing: stop thinking about it.

Our brains are beautiful tools. Astonishing meat computers. Because of them, many people can have light at night and sit in a cool room on a hot day—or a warm room on a cold day. Most people have horseless travel, and some can fly faster than the speed of sound. Humans can travel to the moon, split the atom, and cure diseases that killed millions of people in the past. We have figured out how to feed seven billion people (albeit some better than others). But our individual minds have not discovered the secret to getting what we want and avoiding what we don't want—in other words how to be happy. We struggle with that conundrum our entire lives though the riddle was solved thousands of years ago. It still eludes 99.9 percent of us. Part of the problem of the riddle is that what a person wants or wishes to avoid is different for everyone. But it is only a minor complication and requires looking at the problem differently.

Let's see if I can get closer to the top of this dang pass and then pursue this further.

I was carrying a lot of water up this hill because this was no place to run out. The map convincingly said that there was a rest stop just before the top of the pass on the westbound side. I found no information about water availability there. In fact, the truck driver back at the Cardwell Store said he was pretty sure there wasn't any.

I was wondering what this would be like for someone who was new to this sort of thing. I spent a lot of time in my life heading into the unknown—as we all have. I may have gone a little more out there, so an experience like this is not new to me. Backpacking through third-world countries is a proliferation of unknowns, and that is what I liked. This bicycle odyssey is a milder version of that.

Years ago, I found myself on the island of Borneo. I was traveling with my friend, Debbie, who I had met back in the states. She wanted to see some of the world. She might not have set out on her own, but she was intrepid enough to tag along with me.

We were visiting an orangutan sanctuary in the Malaysian state of Sabah. The Sepilok Orangutan Rehabilitation Centre took in orphaned orangutans that were rescued from logging camps, plantations, and illegal hunting. Often their mothers had been killed for food.

I had learned enough of the language to know that in Malaysia *orang* translated to person and *utan* meant forest.

The compound was very rustic back then. It consisted of a few buildings that housed a small visitor's center and some rangers. There was a path that led into the jungle to a feeding platform set up in a tree.

175

They would feed milk and bananas to the baby apes at the platform. Eventually, the youngsters would grow out of it and foray out into the jungle to look for different opportunities.

The place could not be compared to parks in the United States. There were no boardwalks, no handrails, no gates or barriers, and none of the swarms of safety measures that were present in the litigious United States. When we stepped out of the compound, it was us and the jungle. At prescribed times of the day, tourists followed the rangers to the platform to watch them feed the baby orangutans.

I got the bright idea that it would be interesting to walk out to the platform and see what it was like before the action started. I might have known, but that led to us becoming the action.

I was leading down the path, and when I could see the platform up ahead, the bushes started shaking in front of us. We stopped, and a baby orangutan popped out onto the trail, walking toward me. It raised its hand to me, and I put mine out. The little ape took my hand and then lifted its feet off the ground. Another baby came out and took my other hand and did the same thing. Then two more came out and attached themselves to my shins. I turned around with my four baby orangutans attached and saw Debbie cradling a fifth one. These little apes have such soulful looks in their eyes. It was an amazing experience.

We had only gotten to enjoy this magical encounter for a couple of minutes when the five babies suddenly scattered in alarm. Out came what would amount to an adolescent orangutan. These apes are very human-like in their looks and movements, but for their size they have superhuman strength and agility. After all, they climb trees for a living.

The older one probably weighed about 30 pounds. The only thing soulful about him was the amount of mischief he wanted to get into. He went for my friend, and she turned away from him. In a split second he climbed up her back and was opening the zipper on her backpack with his lips. I knew that no good was going to come of that, and I grabbed his head and started pulling. He let go of her, and I used the leverage to sling him back in the brush. Of course, he came right back out.

I had learned a lot about apes and monkeys in my travels. The primates had educated me. Where wild monkeys and humans meet, the human is the visitor. Your first encounter with a monkey is their thousandth encounter with tourists. You don't know what they are going to do, but they know exactly what you are going to do.

A friend's encounter with a monkey in Indonesia was a case in point. Outside of the reserve, people sold little paper cones of peanuts to feed to the monkeys. We each bought one, and I instinctively tucked mine inside my shirt. I didn't think to warn her. She blithely walked into the sanctuary area, and a mother monkey with a baby attached to her underside ran straight at her, hissing. She threw her peanuts up in the air and ran.

So now I was facing off with this bored teenager who was looking for some action. He walked toward me, eyeing me over. I was crouched down, facing him in a wrestler's stance. I had no idea what he was going to do, but I presumed it would be monkey-like, and I wished I didn't have to take part in it. I know that primates have a predilection for eyeglasses.

He came right up to me and reached up. I grabbed my glasses, and he pulled my hat off my head and ducked away. It was a University of Florida baseball cap. He examined it a little bit and then put it on. I knew the hat was probably gone forever, so it was funny as heck. He aped around a little bit, either imitating or mocking me. Then he took it off and studied it some more. Then he put it on backwards. It was hilarious and would have made an awesome cell-phone video, but cell phones had not been invented yet.

Just before the rangers showed up, he put the hat on the ground and stood on it, and carefully pulled all the seams apart with his teeth. Then he ran off for the feeding.

Well, that was fun for the price of a hat, but I didn't know that he wasn't through with us yet.

A couple of other tourists had joined us, and when the feeding show was over, we walked back down the trail in a line to the compound. Partway back to camp, the adolescent ape was high up in a tree waiting for us. As we got near, he tried to urinate on us. I was kind of surprised that his aim wasn't better. Nobody got wet. When he was out of ammo, he came down the tree and disappeared into the jungle.

A few moments later, he came out of the brush and went straight for Debbie. She was very blonde, and maybe that attracted him. He reached for her. I grabbed his hand and pulled him. He reached for me with his free hand, and I grabbed it. Then he grabbed each of my ankles with his feet.

My height over him gave me a small advantage by leverage. We were otherwise locked up, but then he started to try to bite my knee. These apes do not have the frightening dentition that other primates have, but I was pretty sure that I didn't want to have a personal encounter with these teeth. He kept getting closer to my knee, and all I could do was to lift his arms so he couldn't reach it. It was a frightening calisthenic, and I was losing. Each time he went for my knee, he got closer.

A German woman among us had the presence of mind to open a can of cola and put it on the ground. The ape immediately let go of me and grabbed it. The ransom was paid, and the hostage released. We all left in a hurry with him guzzling his can of soda—rearming for his next batch of tourists.

That was really something and would have made a plenty good story, but my ape encounters still weren't finished.

Back at the compound, I was chilling at the corner of a building feeling lucky that my orangutan experience ended without harm. I was leaned against the building quite relaxed when a ranger came flying around the corner in a dead run with a full-grown, male orangutan in hot pursuit. When the ape saw me just standing there, he stopped.

He was at least 170 pounds and about five feet tall. When the males reach adulthood, they develop these huge, flat faces. It might look good to a female orangutan, but it was terrifying to me.

I imagine he must have thought to himself, "Why isn't this fool running?" I'm sure that he knew that he could do anything he wanted with me, and no one would be able to stop him.

I didn't run because I can't. I could barely outrun a sloth. I stood there and covered my eyes with my hand. I had a lump in my throat the size of a guava. I wondered what Tarzan would do.

It's possible that the only reason he paused was that he couldn't decide which would be more fun: tear my head off or tear my arms off. I'm sure he could have done either without breaking stride.

Just then, a ranger came from behind the far end of the building dragging a stalk of bananas. He dropped it and ran as the ape rushed over and started chowing on bananas. I had just enough time to notice that the orangutan didn't bother to peel the banana. He just squeezed it into his mouth like a Gu packet. I fled.

We had had enough monkeying around at the ape sanctuary, and we left.

CHAPTER 15

Applied Equanimity

The climb to Homestake Pass was relentless. There were no flat spots, no breaks. Given my disability, once I stop on an uphill climb, I cannot get on the bike and start pedaling again. I get off and rest a while, then walk a while and then rest some more. Luckily, there were huge breaks in traffic where I could walk out to the center of the highway—get on the bike—and start at a level angle across the lane and then turn up the hill. After not very far, maybe 100 to 150 yards, I would stop again and do the process all over.

This is where the not-thinking-about-it comes in. When we are faced with a situation, and we call it a problem, we have cast a negative aspersion on it that we would do better without. The situation does not change when we call it a problem—we do. And so does our approach. Negativity never helps and usually makes things worse. This goes for every time we get a negative feeling. I mean, go ahead and have the negative feeling, but at least try to see how it affects the situation. We may not be able to look at it clearly while we are in the middle of it, but at least examine it afterward.

Complaining never helps except to further damage an already-damaged ego. It would help to remember that we are an input into other people's lives. Do we want to lift them up, or do we want to bring them down into our gutter? We have a choice. Most people can't see that there is a choice because they are on stimulus-response autopilot.

With some practice, we can deal with a situation outside of our desire for a particular outcome. We will start dealing with it with a kind of clarity that we might not otherwise embody. We will start to become the change that we want to see in the world. Let's call it applied equanimity.

In this case I am by myself except for the people in cars and trucks rushing by. I couldn't complain to anyone if I wanted to. Nor would I. I still feel lucky. I can list a lot of positive aspects: *as a 69-year-old gimp, I can still tackle something like this. It is pleasantly cool, and I have a slight following breeze. If I can't crest this beast today, I can always put my bicycle and tent on a flat spot on the other side of the guardrail and spend the night. It might not be ideal, but so what? Hmm, SO WHAT might make a good mantra.*

I'm not saying I wasn't wearing down. As I got higher up, I was walking and resting longer and riding less. That's just how I roll. I could look back at the whole valley I had risen out of and marvel at my progress. I found looking forward less marvelous as there was nothing but up.

I had had an experience like this when I was traveling through Nepal. My friend Dave and I were touring in India and had decided to divert to Nepal to "trek" the Annapurna Circuit. It was in 1982, and I was in decent hiking shape back then. I also had an excellent hiking partner who was patient.

The trekking circuit had only been open for five years. It was very different back then. Nepal had not yet figured out that they had a tourism gold mine on their hands. It cost us about $5 each to enter the country, and there were no trekking fees. When we crossed the border, the customs agent, a very kindly, elder gentleman, asked me to pay in Nepalese rupees. We only had Indian rupees. I told him that I could go back across the border to the bank and exchange my rupees. He said OK and then reached in his drawer and pulled out a huge wad of Indian rupees and handed them to me. He asked me if I would change those as well.

The Annapurna Circuit had no roads, no check points, and no communication. The only way to cover the trail was by walking. There were sherpas carrying huge packs on powerful-looking legs and bare, cracked feet. They were the trucks. Using a guide was recommended but not required. A Nepalese man told me that I could hire a porter to carry me if I needed.

We were not well-equipped, but we could rent any gear we needed in Pokara or Kathmandu. Unfortunately, I rented hiking boots that were terribly slippery in snow. I would not make that dismaying discovery until far up the trail.

We left Pokara by bus to a village where we would start the trek. The trail started at about 3,000 feet in elevation, and with good luck, nine days later, we would hit Thorong La, a pass that was 17,769 feet above sea level. That trek was worthy of a book, but the most relevant part was the trouble I got into on the ninth day getting over the pass.

In Pokara we had heard that the pass was not open yet because of snow, but that it would likely be open by the time we got there. Though it was February, and the pass is high elevation, it is often open then. Thorong La sits roughly on the same latitude as Orlando, Florida. So, imagine a 17,000-foot mountain pass on Interstate 4.

We had obeyed the rules for hiking at high elevation. We stayed hydrated and always spent the night at a lower elevation than we had attained that day. The night before going over the pass, there were at least 20 of us trekkers crammed into a little vacant hut. We were about 15,000 feet above sea level, and sleeping was fitful at that altitude. Dave and I intended to leave at five in the morning. One of the rules was, "Don't go if your pulse is over 100 beats per minute." Mine was exactly 100 BPM that morning.

Wisdom would have dictated staying another day or even dropping to a lower elevation and acclimating better. But no, we pushed on. It was dark, and there were snow flurries falling that morning.

As light came on, the snow stopped, but the sky stayed heavily overcast. I was feeling mild altitude sickness. The problem was (there is that word—problem) that every time I hit a patch of snow or tried to go over a hardened snowbank, I fell—several times. Occasionally, we would come to a snow field, and I would fall my way across it. Dave was not having this problem, and he eventually got far ahead of me and out of sight. He was already heroically carrying most of my stuff, and he wasn't feeling well either. On top of thin oxygen and a lot of up to the trail, I had to constantly pick myself up off the ground. After a while, I was falling from pure exhaustion. There seemed to be endless false summits.

My pulse was clicking in my ears way too fast to count. I was getting lightheaded, but I remember lying with my face in the snow thinking that my friends would get to brag that they knew someone who died in the Himalayas.

I was suffering with hypothermia as well. I lay in the snow, knowing that if I went to sleep I would die, and all I wanted to do was go to sleep. I really, honestly no longer cared. I was fine with it.

I lay there in the snow, but after a while, I would find myself getting up—hiking a bit further—and then falling again to lie in the snow. It was not my will. I didn't care. I did not think, "Well, I'd better get going if I'm going to make it." That thought never entered my mind. But then—after some time—I would literally find myself getting up again—as if I was watching someone else. That is how I made it to the top of Thorong La.

Compared to that, this bicycle ascent was a cake walk. I was not delirious, I was not hypothermic, and there was plenty of oxygen. After a lot of stopping and starting again, I came to the portion that went down. That was a bit of a bummer because I knew I was not at the top. I was descending to the "rest stop" that was provided for truckers. It was only a wide area where numerous trucks could stop. It had pit toilets, but as predicted—no water.

There was a man walking his dog back to his semitruck from the grassy, dog area. After he put away his dog, he came over to me. His name was Gary. He had been a cyclist in the past. He was not in a big hurry, so we had an animated and very congenial conversation about biking and trucking, and where we lived and some of our past. We enjoyed an instant rapport.

Somehow, I remembered to ask him if he had any water to spare. I told him that I was pretty sure I had enough to get to the top of the pass provided I didn't meet with any unforeseen travail. He had a spare gallon in his truck, and he topped off my bottles. I didn't know that, from this rest area, it was not a long way to the top.

Later in the trip, I noticed that he had looked up my GoFundMe and donated. Thank you, Gary.

I still had several hundred feet to climb, but I did not realize that I could almost see the top from the rest stop. What a joyous surprise. I was almost finished climbing.

After a bunch more stops and starts, I was at the top. It was a few hours before dark, and I could see no sense in racing down. I could easily make it to Butte, but it was so beautiful up there. The top of

Homestake Pass was a cool, sweet-smelling pine forest with dirt roads running off in different directions. I thought I could easily find an excellent stealth camp. I could see some of Homestake Lake down below. It looked beautiful. It was an image of tranquility with hundreds if not thousands of vehicles raging past not far away.

I didn't want to drop down there and have to climb back up the next day. I followed a dirt road that I could tell was going to take me to a good camping spot without losing a lot of elevation. But when I rounded a corner, I saw that it was already a well-known spot. I rode in on a large family camping circle. There were four or five camper vehicles and trailers of various sizes. Several adults were sitting around a rock campfire circle, and there were a bunch of kids frolicking. There were three dogs, but only one showed signs of caution. The other two didn't seem to care about me.

I had barged in on a family camping gathering. Just as Easter had snuck up on me back in Tallahassee, I had not remembered that this was the Memorial Day weekend. There was nothing to do but ask about the camping availability in the area. I did not even know if I was on state, federal, or private land.

Of course, it was very unusual for a laden bicycle to show up there. They told me that there were no restrictions on camping and that they camped up here a lot. Then someone said the sweetest thing, "Would you like a hamburger?"

What a wonderfully welcoming question. I can still hear it. They probably could not have asked anyone who more wanted a hamburger. I had just ridden and pushed my bike up an 1,800-foot hill over the course of several hours. I said that I'd love one.

I was also happy to get off my bike and sit on a chair. While they were preparing the burger, they asked me another favorite question, "Would you like a beer?" Hmm, same answer.

I was in the camp of a couple from Butte, Montana. They were there with their daughter and numerous grandkids. They were staying up at

Homestake for a while, and several others had left to go to work. They welcomed me in like I was part of the family. It was fun to join them and watch the kids and the dogs play. The cautious dog eventually decided that I was an all-right guy, and we made good friends.

As darkness and cold started to impose on us, they asked me if I would like to spend the night in the pop-up camper. The owners had returned to town for a few days. So now not only did I get two hamburgers and a beer, but I also had an indoor place to spend the night. A fortuitous end to an arduous day!

40 miles.

They offered to put the heat on in the pop-up for me, but I told them I was going straight to bed, and I would be fine in my bag, which I was. But it was very cold at the top of the pass first thing in the morning. I was able to lie around a bit and warm up to the idea of getting up in the cold. Anyway, I did not want to rush out of camp on my new friends.

It was a lovely morning that started warming up as soon as the sun rose in the clear sky. We sat around the campfire and had coffee. After my second cup, I bid them farewell. I had warmed up enough to descend the other side of the pass into Butte.

The drop was even steeper on the back side. I feathered my rear brake until I was afraid it would get too hot, and then I switched to the front brake and feathered it. I swapped back and forth until I felt the brakes had had enough, and I pulled over and let them cool. Why not? Yes, speed is fun, but the faster I went, the more brittle I felt. I guess that is just part of getting old. Besides, I had no deadline and was not in a hurry. I wanted to enjoy the coasting and watching Butte and the amazing open pit mine adjacent to it get closer.

I got off the Interstate on Mount Highland Drive and took it to Elizabeth Warren Avenue. I was quite surprised to see a street in Montana named after Elizabeth Warren, but it turned out to be a different Elizabeth Warren than the one I knew of.

I was targeting the Super Walmart to make some photos for my yard guy. Despite being able to make this bicycle odyssey, I am too gimpy to cut my own grass back home. The fellow who does it for me does not have a good device for receiving pictures, so every now and then, I print some out to send to him. In this Walmart the instant photo machines were out of order, and I had to use the one-hour machines. An hour was not enough time to have the relaxed breakfast I wanted, so I had 60 minutes to kill.

I was surprised and pleased to find a barbershop in this Walmart. I don't remember ever seeing one in a Walmart before. Besides, it was May 31, Memorial Day, and it was open. I was at the end of two months on the road. I needed a haircut.

After getting my photos and a haircut, I was off to a Perkins restaurant down the road. I sat in there enjoying a great big breakfast and catching up on my correspondence. In addition to posting photos on GoFundMe Route 69, I had a bunch of friends and family members who were following me in spirit. I did not engage in any written correspondence except a note with the pictures I was sending to my yard guy and his wife. It's the modern era.

Back in the day, when I traveled to Nepal, my only mode of communication was a letter, which took 13 days to get to the United States. If you had to, you could find a place to make a very expensive, overseas phone call, but that was it. There wasn't even a fax. Nowadays we are carrying phones in our pockets. The world is so much smaller, and I'm happy to have done my overseas traveling when I did. I had ventured into the wilds without the possibility of communication. These days, you can call your mom from any of those far-flung places.

I left Butte on the Blacktail Creek Trail. Blacktail Creek is a very early tributary to the Clark Fork River watershed. This would become important to me later. I did not know it yet, but I would end up riding along the Clark Fork all the way to Idaho.

I traded frontage roads for Interstate. When the road bent to the north, I found myself with a 13 MPH wind straight in my face. At the intersection with Highway 1, I entered a nice rest area with a big "no camping" sign. It was too early to stop for the night, but I was tired of fighting that wind. I sat for quite a while under a flag that was flapping straight out in the wrong direction. It was telling me not to get back on Truckee. I was relieved that my wind app said it would be much better tomorrow.

I was 16 miles from the town of Anaconda, and I could see a giant smokestack cutting into the skyline there. The town would have been on my way, but I had elected not to take Highway 1 toward Missoula because it was narrow, winding and hilly, and it was still Memorial Day weekend. I didn't want to risk it.

I read that the chimney was still the tallest totally masonry construction in the world, as it was when it was first built. There have been taller ones constructed since this one, but they have all been demolished. The giant chimney was constructed in 1918 as part of a copper smelting operation. The largest non-ferrous smelter in the world was closed in 1980. I would like to have visited the structure, but I was not willing to add the 32-mile round trip.

While I was lazing around, I had lots of short conversations with people visiting the rest area. But then a young woman with her partner carrying a child walked up and asked me about my trip. She was keenly interested, and we talked about our biking experiences. She had crossed the country from Los Angeles to Boston on her bike. I could picture our combined routes making a huge X on a map of the United States. She introduced herself, but then added that she worked for the Adventure Cycling Association as their GIS analyst and cartographer.

Wow! That rocked me. My degree at the University of Florida was in geography, and my next targeted stop was Missoula to visit the Adventure Cycling Association. I felt like I was meeting a celebrity. We talked about biking and routes, and what it was like for them biking with a small child. There is a kinship among XC cyclists, even if they are no longer doing cross-country rides.

They moved on, and I went about some bicycle maintenance. I was sitting on the ground, but when I tried to get up using my cane, I lost my balance and fell backward. I landed very hard with the rigid cane between the cement and my "sit" bone. The pain was excruciating. If you don't know what a sit bone is, get a bicycle seat that doesn't fit well and ride it for a while. The sit bone will announce itself quickly. I crawled over and tried to sit on a bench. I could only do it if I leaned way over to stay off the injury. I almost had to lie down. I didn't think I broke anything, but I knew I had done some real damage to something. Pain, pain, pain! I had slammed some poor part of myself between the round aluminum cane and bone... throb...

Now what? Could I have someone look at it? A random rest area visitor? I'm sure they'd be thrilled. Could I still ride my bike? Was my cycling odyssey going to be ended here by an ignoble butt injury? I had traveled over 2,900 miles! I only had two or three weeks left!

I waited until very close to dark, and then I painfully laid out my sleeping stuff on the narrow cement slab behind the building. I didn't set the tent up but instead just threw it over me for some protection from the wind. The breeze was lying down nicely with the darkness.

I'm sure there are medical people in Anaconda. It has a population over 9,000. But I wasn't going to ride there tonight anyway. Maybe tomorrow.

I telephoned my wife for medical advice. By now, I had a hard inflammation that felt like another bone under my skin. She told me to massage it as hard as I could until it was too painful, then stop. And then repeat it.

I did that until about 10 p.m. I had now been on the road for two months. I wondered if I was going to be able to ride my bike at all tomorrow. I fell asleep massaging my painful injury.

35 miles.

I slept until 7 a.m. I took my time getting up because I was in no hurry to find out that my odyssey was finished. The massaging had helped a lot, but the spot was still extremely painful to touch. I would not know if massaging the injury helped enough until I sat on the bicycle seat. A butt injury back in Mississippi could have ended the trip without much grief, but almost 3,000 miles later, it would be a harder loss to surmount. I walked around for a while and massaged the painful spot. Finally, it was time to face up to it: either I could ride, or I couldn't.

I walked the bike into the parking lot. Thankfully, it wasn't very busy. I stepped on the pedal, pushed, and swung my leg over. Even that hurt.

As I rolled and lowered myself onto the saddle, I found that it was quite painful. But the injury was to the outside edge of my sit bone. I pedaled some, and the pain did not increase. I was going to be able to ride. I was lucky by millimeters.

I rolled out onto Interstate 90. My pain and I got into the rhythm of riding the bicycle. At the Warm Springs exit, I was able to get onto the frontage road and ride it all the way into Deer Lodge.

The claim to fame of Deer Lodge is the Montana State Prison and the Old Prison Museum. I stopped at the Kaffeination Station for breakfast. It was a classy place to coffee up with some inside seating.

I was finding out, though, that sitting on chairs or benches was quite delicate with an awkward amount of leaning involved. I had injured the "sit" out of myself.

The young lady that owned the place was a cyclist. She was not a cross-country biker, but she put down some impressive mileage on day rides. I really enjoyed talking with her and the crew.

When I was ready to leave, I asked for an iced coffee to go. It was going to be hot riding now. The owner gave me a complimentary iced coffee.

It was difficult to tell where I would be able to get anything next. I planned to follow the Interstate for 10 more miles and then turn off onto Highway 12. I would go back roads the rest of the way to Missoula. I couldn't tell on my maps or apps where dependable services might be.

On the way out of town, I stopped at the post office to mail the photos to my lawn guy. I had noticed a shortcut on the map that I could take to cut over to Highway 12. I asked inside about that shortcut, but the counter person didn't know. A guy followed me outside and stopped me. He wanted to know about the biking. We talked for a while. He said that I would be happy with the route to Missoula I was planning, but he wasn't sure if the shortcut was good for a bicycle or not.

I rode on a frontage road for 14 miles to Beck Hill Road, which was my shortcut road. I was happy to get away from the Interstate, and this five-mile-long shortcut would save about seven miles. GMB wanted me to take it, but I was wary.

I didn't listen to my intuition, and I went up Beck Hill Road because at least it was paved. This was supposed to be some kind of cross-country adventure anyway… right?

The road turned steeply uphill just before the pavement ended. I had only gone about a mile, but now it would feel like defeat to turn around. I kept going, walking the bike a lot. My "sit" injury was annoying, but it was not going to stop me.

The terrain was dry and scenic. There was the odd house and not much else. I was up high and could see way back down the Interstate.

It turned out there were very few places that I could ride because it was too steep. After a lot of pushing, I reached the top, but then I couldn't ride down except at dead slow—brakes all the way. The little rocks in the dirt were like ball bearings, so it was difficult to keep the bike upright. It was a slow, harrowing descent. I surely didn't want to add any other injuries.

At the bottom I crossed a railroad track, the Little Blackfoot River, and got on Highway 12. The shortcut was a mistake. It was a shortcut by distance only. I could easily have gone the long way in half the time and would not have risked crashing. Thank you, GMB. Once again it would have been great on a mountain bike carrying nothing, but it was a little slice of hell to this touring biker. My love/hate relationship with Google Maps Bicycle continued.

I was off to Avon. According to my apps, there were no services there. Highway 12 was not as quiet as I expected, but with a closer inspection of my paper map, I saw that anyone in Helena wanting to go west was going to be on this road. It was a good road with a small shoulder, and a pleasant nine miles to Avon where I had to turn northwest on Highway 141.

As I made that turn, my bicycle would not downshift to the low gear on the front sprocket. It was a critical malfunction, as this was my most-used gear-range across the entire country. I don't have the strength in my legs to go without those lower gears.

As far as I could tell, Avon was just a collection of houses at this intersection. I pulled into the shade alongside someone's fence.

I couldn't see anything wrong with the derailleur, but it was difficult to adjust without being able to suspend my rear wheel off the ground. I would have to find some kind of shop or another person—at least a rope and a tree. If I couldn't find a way to repair it in Avon, Helena was 30 miles away. I was sure I could hitch there if I had to.

I got back on the road and toured the small collection of houses. I came across a woman dropping another woman off at home. I asked them if they knew anyone in town that was a cyclist. They said that the people that ran the café were into cycling.

Café?! My apps said there were no services! I asked where the café was, and they said it was just a little way in the other direction on Highway 12. I rode over there, and my bicycle shifted just fine. I couldn't explain it quitting, and I couldn't explain it working again.

The café was by no means a new addition to town. It had clearly been there before these apps were invented. I don't know why neither of my map apps knew about it. It is one of the reasons that an ACA map is wonderful to travel with if one is on an ACA route. But I wasn't, and the Avon Family Café was a great discovery.

I explained my predicament to the waitress. She said that neither of the owners were there at the time, but she would be happy to try calling them. In my usual modus operandi, I asked her to wait on the call, and I ordered a Spanish omelet. "Breakfast all day" is one of my favorite phrases. As I ate, I thought that since the bike seemed to be working now, I could start my ride out of town and return if I had to.

I left Avon and rode into hill-and-dale countryside. Bucolic. The area was dedicated to cows and growing cow food. It was spare of trees. Pastoral. I could top the hills even though the wind was slightly against me. The traffic wasn't bad, though there was more than I would expect cutting through this rural area. The only thing ahead was the Scapegoat Wilderness and the Lolo National Forest. Maybe everyone was headed for the Rattlesnake Wilderness National Recreation Area. It seemed unlikely. At any rate I was again participating in some beautiful countryside. You can't beat the western states for majesty.

When the time came to find a hideout, the only places with good tree cover were on steep hillsides that I would be unable to negotiate. One aspect of stealth camping is passing a decent place while looking for a better place, and then having to settle for something less. I was on a series of curves on a hillside and running out of steam. Around each curve I was hoping for something better, and I did this for a couple miles before finally doing a rare backtracking maneuver for a mediocre spot. It was on a sharp curve barely behind a few trees. I had to dig a flat spot for my tent out of the steep scree slope. It broke a rule of mine not to alter any landscape, never mind that the nearest structure I could see was a ranch five or six miles away.

The plain far below my campsite was treeless and dotted with cows. The sky was clear, and the sun was setting. My quietude was interrupted by a pickup truck stopping just below my hillside encampment. What now!? The driver got out with a pair of binoculars. He perused the landscape below for a few minutes, and as he got back in his vehicle, he gave me a little wave. I guess he was just checking on his cows.

30 miles.

CHAPTER 16

Exquisite Veracities

I woke up feeling refreshed. Next stop Ovando. It was the next likely service and about 17 miles away. I crossed the Blackfoot River just before getting on Highway 200. The highway followed the Blackfoot to Missoula. The town of Ovando was mostly off Highway 200, and the first thing I came to was Trixi's Antler Saloon. It was also the only thing out by the highway. It was very sunny out and starting to get hot. Trixi's was dark like a cave. When I stepped inside and my eyes adjusted, I could see the rustic decor and the ubiquitous Montana slot machines. I sat at the end of the bar and was told I had missed breakfast by 15 minutes. Dang! Okay, cheeseburger, fries, water.

The waitress/bartender was a vivacious young woman. I asked her if she was Trixi. She wasn't. Since my biking outfit was obvious, she asked me about my trip. She was shocked that I had ridden to her saloon from Florida. We were instantly pals, and although she was busy, she made time to talk about my trip. She asked me how old I was but was called away before I could answer. Hey, Trixi, I was 69 when we met.

I left Ovando in the bright, clear sun. I bumped into the Blackfoot River again during the 14 miles to the intersection with Highway 83. The river was growing with spring-thaw water. Rivers are magic, and I am always enchanted by them. With water you live; without it you don't. It is such a beautiful, truthful, sublime metric.

The time it takes to cover distances on a bicycle is time existing in these simple, exquisite veracities. Maybe that should be the answer to the question why I am making a trip like this.

Earlier on, I alluded to the "riddle of happiness." We spend the greatest portion of our lives looking to get happy. We think, "If I get this, I will be happy—if I avoid that I will be happy." Over time, the this's and that's change, which leads to a lifetime of clutching and clawing. "I want a Barbie… I want a new car… I want better health." The breadth of desire is as expansive as it is unquenchable.

What if we were already happy but covering it up with a never-ending list of things we want or want to avoid? What if we were shown from an early age that it is the wanting that blocks our own light of happiness from us? The answer to these two questions leads us to the most exquisite of veracities. We can feel joy all the time if we can just get out of our own way. No one else need be involved.

I am not talking about a goofy sense of giddiness. I am talking about a natural, sublime joy with which to face every situation—an essence to have as a keystone. The salient answer to the riddle is there in all of us, but most of us only visit it on rare occasion.

There was a Sinclair gas station at the intersection with Highway 83 along with Stoney's Kwik-stop Lounge and Casino. 83 goes north to Flathead Lake. I have a friend north of there in Kalispel, and I bet that is a beautiful highway with lots of excellent camping opportunities. If I was not determined to visit the Adventure Cycling Association Headquarters in Missoula, I would have gone that way… next time.

Stoney's had some picnic tables in the shade, and I got a coffee and rested there for quite a while. A fellow from Alabama came over, and we enjoyed a long conversation. When we were done, he went in and bought a bottle of water for me. These chitchats and nice gestures really make a bike trip—very much a part of the "exquisite veracities."

Down the road, I crossed the Clearwater River that was on its way to merge into the Blackfoot. I crossed the Blackfoot again in a few miles. Seven miles from Highway 83, I was at the turnoff for the town of Greenough, but I didn't take it. I was still well-watered and had good energy, but I did not know what a climb I had ahead of me.

It was an unexpected slog. Not the most difficult I'd had—getting over the divide took that honor. But I did not see this one coming. After all, I was supposedly traveling downstream. And I had another one coming, again, where I didn't expect it.

There were areas steep enough that the road branched out to include a passing lane for the automobile traffic. I was pedaling up the hill and having to walk and stop for regular rests. Walking the bike is almost as restful as just standing. I finally came to a sign that indicated the passing lane was ending. Always good news for the cyclist. Then came the sign that depicted a stylized truck going down a steep hill. Most excellent news for this old guy on his bike. From that point on, except for one flat area, it would be downhill all the way to Missoula. Did I mention how much I love coasting?

Highway 200 crossed the Blackfoot River, and now I was traveling with the river close on my left. I thought there would be good places to quit early for the day, but private property and inaccessible landscape prevailed. I finally came to a public access to the river where a "no camping" sign glared at me. I pushed Truckee on a brushy, narrow path over small hills to the river.

It was beautiful and a perfect place to camp. There was a little eddy from the river torrent right in front of me. I had been looking forward to checking in to the next cheap motel that I came to because

I wanted to be fresh the next day when I visited the Adventure Cycling Association office. After all, this was day seven since my last shower back in Laurel. But while I sat there with my bare feet in the ice-cold water, I figured that I could just have a sponge-bath here, camp somewhere for the night, and save the motel room expense. There were some people upstream of me barely in sight and a couple people downstream also behind some bushes. I took off everything but my biking shorts and had a wonderful, freezing-cold wash-up. Somewhere upstream this water had recently been snow.

I was radically invigorated and darkness was coming, but I did not feel I could camp there. It was too populated to be stealthy. The person upstream had left, but the people downstream were still there. It didn't feel right, so I left. I was too far into civilization to find an excellent stealth camp. Now I just had to find something before I got even further into developed area.

I came upon a well-traveled gravel road on the uphill side of the highway. There was nothing in the immediate area, but there were "no trespassing" signs. Rather than go up the road and see if I could get permission from someone to camp, I pushed Truckee back into the woods and covered it with my tarp. I didn't want the reflective bits on my bike to give away my position in case headlights came down the road. The area was nice and dry, so I didn't need the tarp as a ground cloth. I didn't like camping behind "no camping" signs, nor did I like camping behind "no trespassing" signs, but in a pinch, it is another truth that forgiveness is easier to get than permission.

I would have to get a motel tomorrow in Missoula to do laundry. It would be a short riding day. After having gotten cleaned up, I had an excellent, restful night. At some point today, I crossed the 3,000-mile mark.

68 miles.

I got a first light start for my 14-mile ride into Missoula. I had been keeping my eye out for a breakfast spot on the way in, but I ended up getting all the way into town without finding one. I rode to East Pine Street to have a look at the ACA office. I confirmed that they welcomed cyclists starting at 10 a.m. Perfect.

I rode further into the downtown and had breakfast at the Catalyst Café. Even though they had some nice tables outside, I took one inside. They weren't quite as COVID-paranoid as I would have expected. I guess their prohibition on inside seating had just ended. It was a very nice place with excellent food and service.

As I was leaving, some people at one of the tables outside asked me about my loaded bike. The people at another table chimed in on the conversation, and then a couple of passersby joined the discussion. The loaded bicycle was like a magnet sometimes. By this time, people who I told my story to declared that I was inspiring. I was hearing it every time.

I thought about what this meant in terms of my traveling. I did not set out to be an inspiration to anyone. I set out in my joy to see if I could ride my bicycle to Port Townsend, Washington. I never dreamed I would end up writing this book. I just set out to see if I could make the trip. Being inspirational is just an awesome side effect of doing something interesting and different.

There is an essence to this undertaking that is an essence to my whole life. It is an essence that cannot be expressed in words. That essence was what got my body out of the snow of its own accord in the Himalayas. The same thing that kept me from drowning in my canoe accident. The essence was with me at birth, and I am lucky to already see that it will be with me at death no matter the manner. I could throw a word at it like love or God and bury it from sight in doing so. Words block the light from us.

For all the lives of most of us, we only pay attention to our thoughts, our feelings, and the signals that come in through our senses. It would be difficult to convince most people that they could experience anything else. There is an ocean, but we spend most of our time splashing around in the shallows. Swim out... dive down. Find out that your thoughts, your ego mind, your words are hiding the essence from you. Your feelings, your sensitivities make it all but impossible to see; your attention to environmental inputs is attention taken away from the essence. Instead of splashing in the kiddy pool of occasional and fleeting happiness, dive into the ocean of rapture, equanimity, and bliss. The atman, the soul. These words are just that... and fall woefully short of what they are trying to describe.

I left the impromptu breakfast club and rode back to the Adventure Cycling Association office. It is really a fun association to be a part of if one is cycling cross-country. Each day, they have a greeter to take cyclists in. They had soda and ice cream and a spotless lounge area and restrooms with a shower. They were expecting me because the woman who I met outside of Anaconda, Montana had texted them that I was coming. They always take pictures of people who stop by, and some get put in the magazine. They even have a scale for weighing a loaded bike, but first they ask how much the rider thinks it weighs. My bike and gear weighed 175 pounds, but I was completely out of food and water at that point. Missoula was a stock-up spot.

While I was talking, I must have mentioned that I needed a paper map of Washington State. Before long, someone handed me a note with the address of a shop that said they had one. The perfect tourist map of Washington. Awesome.

The folks at Adventure Cycling had a list of cheap places to stay, but I was already in the get-back-on-the-road mode. I picked up the needed Washington map from a lovely young gal who said she was excited to meet me for what I was doing. Then, of course, I headed to a Starbucks to look the map over and get a giant iced coffee. It was an unseasonable 100 degrees that afternoon. This high temperature came on the heels of snow the week before.

I made several supply stops on my way to the Super 8 motel. I picked that place for the guest laundry, and I was there early enough to get all my wash done before dinner. I was going to have a really fresh start leaving Missoula.

Missoula was a splurge stop after seven days on the road since my last motel. I had hit the goal of stopping at the ACA headquarters after leaving Florida 64 days ago. Passing 3,000 miles was a pretty cool milestone as well.

I did not want to get back on the bike once I had it in the motel room. There was a place to eat across the street, which I could get to with my cane. It was much fancier looking than any place I would normally frequent, but it was the only thing I could walk to. Besides, wasn't I splurging?

The Montana Club was quite busy for a Thursday evening. I was there early because I wanted to get in bed early. Rather than take up a table in the dining room, I sat at a large table in the bar where I could welcome company. I ordered a large glass of the darkest beer they had while I looked over the menu. I had promised myself to not pay any mind to whatever prices I encountered. Left side of the menu only, close my eyes, and pull the trigger.

I was craving steak still. This would be my third of the trip after not eating steak for a decade. I ordered the most expensive New York Strip I've ever had with a baked potato and a Caesar salad. I ordered another dark beer while waiting for my extravagance to arrive as a threesome of people asked if they could share my table.

Steve and his wife were in town from the Seattle area. They were visiting a relative who was ill, and it seemed it might have been a bummer trip for them. Steve sat closest to me—it was a table that could have seated eight. We talked on and on mostly about my biking across the whole country. The ladies were involved in the discussion though they had to speak through Steve. The din in the bar kept me from hearing them. They were amazed that such an old guy was riding a bike that far. I told them that I felt extremely lucky to have the opportunity and ability to do it.

After my meal, in keeping with the pace of immoderate consumption, I ordered a double Jack Daniel's Tennessee Fire for dessert. My last indulgence. One was enough. I had to make it back to my room. In the last two months, I had had an occasional beer. This was a bit over the top for me.

I asked for the check, and the waiter said, "It's been taken care of." !!! Steve and his party had covered it! Such generosity! Their company had already been a pleasure for me. I thanked them profusely and tottered back over to the Super 8.

25 miles.

Despite my unusual night, I was the first person at the continental breakfast. I coffeed up, ate, and got out the door. There were little spots of rain blowing through, and I kept my eye on the weather radar in hopes of avoiding any downpours. GMB got me out of town without my having to get on the Interstate. About 10 miles out of town, rain became unavoidable. I was traveling on the Frenchtown frontage road when I had to stop and put on my rain gear. The cool weather you would expect in the area this time of year was back, and I didn't want to get wet.

I turned in at a dirt road that passed under I-90. I figured I would just sit there until the precipitation passed. It looked from the radar picture like it would be less than an hour.

A guy in a blue pickup truck came from the other side of the Interstate and stopped where I was sitting. He asked me if I was alright. How nice of him to ask. Yes, I was fine.

We got into the usual conversation about my trip, but that branched into what his sons were doing. He was a local but had lived elsewhere in his life. We had an affable conversation for 20 or 30 minutes, and then he handed me a $20 bill and left. More unsolicited generosity. What a trip!

It stopped raining soon after he left, and I got back on the frontage road. I came to an interchange where Larry's Six Mile Casino and Café was on the other side of the Interstate. I rode over to see what kind of food they might have. It turned out that Larry wasn't there, nor was anyone else, and there was no indication why they might be closed. Too bad because what I needed most was advice. The frontage road was going to end two miles ahead, but there would be a very long long cut that could keep me off of the Interstate. Otherwise, I would have to get on the Interstate now. GMB recommended the long cut, and if it was paved, it sounded good and was likely very scenic.

I invested the two miles and then turned up the long cut. Up it was. Up and up. I didn't care for gaining elevation when I didn't have to, but I felt committed. It was gorgeous country with numerous ranchette-style residences. My commitment faltered after about four miles when the pavement ended. The dirt road was good, but it was still going steeply up. I did not know where I was, but I knew I was nowhere near the point that the road was supposed to reconnect with I-90. Would the dirt road turn to track like it had on me back in the Mississippi Delta and elsewhere? Would I come to a "bridge out" sign like I had twice before? If I was on flat ground, I would have taken the risk, but instead I turned around.

Okay, 10 miles wasted. The worst part was the two miles going east on the frontage road before I got to the interchange that let me get on the Interstate to go west. My earplugs and I were ready.

I only had to travel for a few miles on the Interstate before I was able to get off again on paved frontage road. As I was getting closer to Alberton, I saw the Clark Fork River off to my left. I didn't know it at this time, but I was going to become very familiar with the course of this beautiful river.

In Alberton I rode through to the far end of town in search of repast. I noticed that they had two bars in this small town. I thought that the accompanying small population here must take turns to support the two tiny taverns.

I ended up back at the Valley Grocery. It was a small-town grocery having a little bit of everything. The woman in charge was very helpful in getting me some food and coffee. There was no seating around, and she pointed out a small park that had a restroom back down the road.

As I walked out of the place, there was a pickup truck with a giant dog head sticking out of the passenger window. I asked the woman who had just gotten out of the driver's side if I could say hello to her dog. She said yes and that they were friendly. As I approached I saw another giant dog head squeeze out of the passenger side window to greet me. They were Burnese Mountain Dogs, and they were very friendly. She invited me around to the back of her truck to show me two more giant dogs.

I got my "dog fix" and headed down to the park. The road through town was high above the Interstate Highway and the river. The railroad was on the other side of the river as well.

This lovely scene had been the site of the largest chemical spill from a train in the history of the United States. Back in 1996 a train hauling chlorine derailed on the tracks below. Over 300 people were injured from inhaling chlorine, and a thousand people were evacuated from the area. Interstate 90 was closed for 19 days.

I was there on a very warm day, and having had my extra 10 miles of exercise, I stretched my rolled-up mat out in the grass and had a delicious nap. No travail now except for residual pain lingering from my butt injury.

After my nap, I left town and hooked back up with the frontage road. In five miles the frontage road ended at West Mountain Creek Road. GMB told me that just up the hill there was a road that would take me all the way to Superior, staying off I-90. There were indications that this might be a GMB fantasy, but my only recourse would have been to ride back to Alberton and get on the Interstate there. Once again, facing the unknown versus backtracking, I forged ahead. The paved road was just steep enough that I had to get off and push before it made the expected turn. In a few hundred feet, the pavement ended, but it was now a good, firm dirt road. I was going down a slight grade, but I was losing confidence faster than I was losing elevation. I knew that if I had to turn around, I would be riding this loaded bike up hill. I failed my instincts once again and kept going.

I came to a fence with a walk-through opening. There were some interpretive signs about flora and fauna. I continued even though I was now on what used to be a road. Then that turned into a single track... a foot path. GMB said keep going. I had traveled so far downhill that I knew I didn't want to turn around. I was far above the Interstate so there were only two choices, and the forging ahead choice led downhill.

I came to a tunnel that was closed. There was a foot path leading around it, and I assumed the not-road would continue on the other side. I walked my bike over the stony path. In my youth I would have explored the tunnel further, but now I was busy wondering where in the heck I was and what I had gotten myself into.

The interpretive signs ended, and the used-to-be-road continued. I doubt that it had been used in the last half century. Further on, I came upon a barbed-wire fence that stretched across the road with no gate and a "no trespassing" sign.

GMB didn't seem to know about this impasse. It wanted me to continue just as it had back in Mississippi where there was no bridge to cross the muddy ravine. I leaned the bike against the fence and sat on a rock for some contemplation.

I was extremely glad that Google Maps provided bicycle routes that found bike paths and avoided traffic. It had helped me countless times getting through urban areas. But I wondered how route filtering lets situations like this occur. This has not been a viable route for a very long time except perhaps for covered wagons.

You might ask—with a hint of sarcasm, "where is your essence now?" I can safely say that it was beautifully, exquisitely, and assuredly right where I was sitting. This is one of those situations that can be made into a problem in one's mind. Sure, I could get mad at Google Maps and whoever or whatever else I thought was to blame—including myself. But to waste energy being angry is laughable. In essence, the only thing to do is whatever I would do whether angry, frustrated, or not. So why not leave out the anxiety? As I have said, it never helps.

I started to take the panniers off Truckee. I knew I did not want to push the bike back up the miles I had just traveled downhill. I had to get everything over the barbed-wire to continue. I would take my chances with the trespassing bit. I figured that anyone encountering me would see my pathetic, gimpy ass limping my bike over this track and take pity. Or maybe they would fear me for being insane. What I feared more was running into angry cattle. I could imagine coming across an irate bull protecting his harem. I wondered if my dog spray would be efficacious. I hoped I did not have to find out.

Getting the bike and all my stuff over the barbed wire was easier than getting myself over, but I managed. I reassembled my gear and continued down the non-road. It was road-like, but clearly had not been used on this side of the fence either. It was still a shallow downgrade, and I could tell by the din that I was descending to the Interstate level. It was a lovely, wooded area.

I came upon one steer that was probably perplexed, but he just stood there and watched me pass. I saw a residence through a break in the berm that was beside me. Staying unseen made more sense than trying to explain myself.

Finally, I came to a gate—the kind just held up by a wire loop thrown over a post. Thankfully, there was no bicycle disassembly required. I dropped the gate, pushed the bike through, and put the gate back up. It had opened onto a little road that led back to my old pal Old Highway 10. I crossed the Clark Fork River on an old cement bridge that looked like it might crumble out from under me.

I was able to travel on paved road through some pleasant, wooded terrain. It would have been a terrific area to camp, but there was too much light left for me to stop.

CHAPTER 17

Awesome Route Change

I came upon a fellow who was unloading some heavy equipment from a large trailer. He was an affable guy who said his family had been in the area for seven generations. He was a wonderful atlas of knowledge about the region. I asked him about the route ahead. He warned me that GMB was about to put me on another bridge that did not exist anymore.

I told him I intended to shadow Interstate 90 into Spokane, but he inspired a major course correction. He said he was not a bike rider, but he recommended following the Clark Fork River to Sandpoint—that was all downhill. The ride to Spokane from Sandpoint would be good. The quality of his speech instilled confidence in me. He said there were two steep passes on the Interstate that I would not enjoy. It turned out to be excellent advice.

I rode to Superior, Montana in time for dinner. I ordered dinner with a salad at Durango's. It was a nice-enough place, and my waitress was very young—probably a high school student. She brought my dinner without the salad. When I managed to get her attention again, she brought me the salad she had "forgotten," but then didn't wait around to see what kind of dressing I wanted. She was just young.

I pulled a few miles out of town on the next route GMB suggested and camped in the woods for the night.

69 miles.

I guess I still hadn't learned my lesson. I got an early start in the morning on GMB's route. It was not a good touring-bike road but would have been an excellent mountain-bike road. It turned to a dirt/small-gravel road that climbed and climbed where I didn't need to. On the downhill portions the small gravel again acted like ball bearings. It was very slow going. Had I taken the Interstate, I'm sure I would have been in St. Regis in less than a third of the time. Good thing I was not in a hurry. But I really didn't need the extra workout after having spent more than two months riding my bicycle.

The St. Regis Travel Center was newer and had a trout aquarium and other tourist needs: "Montana's Largest Gift Shop" and "it all." But all I wanted was breakfast, so I pulled into Jasper's Restaurant next door on Old Mullan Gulch Road. I'd had a big morning workout, and I was quite happy to be having breakfast in St. Regis. The vagaries of Highway 135 lay ahead, and it was again going to be difficult to determine what services would be available and where.

There was one couple at another table in my section. I thought it was quite odd that the music in the restaurant was from the late 60s: early Beatles, Herman's Hermits. When I thought I might be the only person there that was familiar with the music, the couple engaged me in conversation. The lady said she knew the songs from when she was in sixth grade. We gleefully discussed that era, and then they asked me about the bike. They were amazed and had lots of questions about the whole trip. They were engaged and engaging. I was happy to sit and have coffee with them. They asked several questions revolving around what I would do if I got in trouble. I told them that I just had to cross that bridge when I came to it. We laughed at the irony of me getting into trouble when I came to an expected bridge that wasn't there. I said I had taken good care of Truckee and decent care of myself, so come what may.

We left Jasper's at the same time. They went to their car, and I readied Truckee for our trip following the Clark Fork River down to the town of Paradise.

I felt a tap on my shoulder. My fellow patron from the restaurant smiled and handed me some folded money. He said, "In case of an emergency." I joked that I might buy an emergency beer with it later. He laughed and said, "Do what you want." I did not look in my hand before they left. When I did look, I saw he had given me a $100 bill! I turned to look for them to thank them better, but they were gone. …Thank you!

The St. Regis-Paradise Scenic Byway is a cycling dream. At least to me it was doing it in this direction. It is 22 miles downhill through forest with only a few collections of houses. The road is excellent with a generous shoulder the entire way. There is a railroad track following along the river, and I could not help but wonder if the engineers, like those along the Yellowstone River, ever got tired of the scenery. There were lots of places to access the river for what had to be terrific rafting and fishing adventures. There were endless stealth camping opportunities where I didn't need any. I felt grateful for having run into the guy loading heavy equipment yesterday who steered me to this route.

It also opened an opportunity for another targeted stop. I had not met my wife's brother's wife's brother before, but when she told him about my cross-country adventure, he asked her to offer a place to stay if I was near Sandpoint, Idaho. Previously I had not intended to pass through Sandpoint, but now it was in my sights. I was looking forward to meeting Ed.

I crossed the Clark Fork River and ran into Highway 200. Just before the town of Paradise, the Flathead River ran into the Clark Fork, making it the biggest river in Montana. I would be following the Clark Fork all the way until it dumped into Lake Pend Oreille.

I was traveling northwest on Highway 200, and unfortunately, there came a strong westerly wind. I stopped for something to eat in Paradise, Montana more for the stop than the eat. I was tired of fighting the wind and relished a chance to get inside and out of it. I had that beat-up feeling.

The meal was the worst food I had gotten on the trip. Let's just say it was unfortunate and leave it at that. It did nothing to assuage the thumping I had taken from the abusive wind. There was an ice cream store in Plains, and I thought I would go there in another attempt to mitigate my physical suffering. The weather was certainly hot enough to suggest ice cream.

It was Saturday, and when I got to Plains, it looked like everyone in town had the same idea. There were a lot of people sitting around outside with ice cream cones and such, but the inside was a bit chaotic. There were four very young people behind the counter, and I joined a long line that was not moving. Someone had gotten something that they hadn't asked for, and all four of the counter kids were trying to work out the problem. As much as I would have liked an ice cream, I thought the Second Coming was more likely than me getting one there.

Despite a few disappointments in that valley, I could not say enough good about the scenery along the route. The Clark Fork River runs between two mountain ranges—the Cabinet Mountain Range and the Coeur d'Alene Range. The valley is somewhat narrow and funneling a stiff wind on me. I left Plains and bore down, albeit slowly, on Thompson Falls.

On my first trip across the country, I got wind-stranded just outside of Marfa in West Texas. The wind was so strong in my face that I could not pedal against it, and I stopped at a tiny rest area. There were two picnic tables each under a shelter roof and nothing else. It would have been the only shade for hundreds of square miles without going back to Marfa. The next available water was 36 miles away in Valentine, and I knew the water I had would not get me that far if I rode against this wind. My sanctuary was buffeted all day without let up, and I stayed at that rest area reading and napping. My wind app said the wind was going to lie down completely at dark.

Late in the afternoon, a cyclist came rocketing into the rest area with the wind behind him. I knew his joy. He had plenty of water and topped me off. Marfa was just minutes away for him.

I left my sanctuary as the sun was setting. The wind quit as predicted, and I had a glorious night ride into Valentine. I had only used two of my seven liters of water. I topped off at a spigot behind the post office in Valentine—slept a few hours behind a church—and rode the rest of the 72 miles to Van Horn. It was a moonless, calm, and even chilly night. The starry desert sky was indescribably beautiful. There was no traffic!

I spent the next windy day in town, and that night, I rode the 67 miles to Fort Hancock under calm conditions. It was an excellent way to beat the torrid, desiccating winds.

Night riding conditions were not presenting themselves this time. About 10 miles short of Thompson Falls, I found a really nice place for a stealth camp. It was in a grassy, open, wooded area up from the road. I was only guessing at the distance to Thompson Falls—I was out of cell phone service. That meant I had to put my rainfly on the tent, and the whole operation was more challenging in the wind.

57 miles.

I had set the alarm for 5 a.m. in hopes of beating the rising wind, but it was already blowing like heck through my hideout. I lay around a while, and by the time I had broken camp, the wind calmed down. The ride into Thompson Falls was pleasant. I hauled into Minnie's Montana Café for breakfast. Sitting at the counter, I had a nice conversation with a local guy. He left for work, and before I finished breakfast, another guy took his place at the counter next to me. What followed was the oddest conversation of my trip. He was an average-looking guy, but he made me start to wonder how far I might be from Hayden Lake, the neo-Nazi Mecca. His questions were much more like a cross-examination than a friendly chat about travel. He did not bring up race, religion, or politics, but it was about as discomfiting an interchange as one could have without broaching those subjects. There was nothing amicable about it. He left in an air of vexation without purchasing anything. That kind of seriousness is born of deep fear, and it is amazing to me that an old man riding his bike across the country could evoke that much apprehension. I would call that guy Caligula squared. Perhaps he was reacting to the rarity of the situation. At any rate it looked like frightful unhappiness born of a runaway mind.

It was sunny and calm when I left Minnie's. I was on the western side of the Clark Fork now. The road moved away from the river, and for a very long way, it was straight as could be. It was a longer straightaway than anything I had experienced in Montana. I was amazed at this unexpected forthright highway.

In Trout Creek I stopped at Nin's Local Store and had a snack and a coffee at their picnic table. A gentleman walked up and asked me about the bike trip, and in a short while, his wife joined him. They were locals. They warned me that there was a bad length of road near the border with Idaho: a wall of rock on one side of the road and a drop-off down to the railroad tracks on the other with no shoulder. They highly recommended that, since it was Sunday, I should get that stretch behind me while traffic was light.

I did not have to hear that twice. I was now determined to make it to Clark Fork, Idaho before dark. It was 39 miles away, and there was a threat of rain. I was pretty sure there were not going to be any more services. The next two towns before the border, Noxon and Heron, were both across the river from Highway 200. I wasn't going to cross those bridges if I didn't have to. Getting to Clark Fork was the new imperative.

GMB wanted me to cross over at Noxon and go all the way to Clark Fork on that side of the river. In hindsight I probably should have done that, but coming off two recent GMB disasters only days ago, I just couldn't do it. I stayed on Highway 200. I knew it would be paved all the way.

After the turnoff for Noxon, a diesel pickup truck slowed near me and then gunned it. This has the effect of blowing out a huge cloud of black diesel exhaust. Unless it is windy, which it wasn't, the cyclist has little choice. If you stop, you are in the middle of it, and if you keep riding, you have to ride through a dissipating cloud of stench. This was my second highway Caligula. Not bad… 1,600 miles per Caligula. On my first trip across country, I had three of these experiences, so that was one per thousand miles.

Other than that wretched fellow, the ride to Clark Fork was good. There were some little rain encounters that did not require donning rain gear. There were very tight places in the road that the couple in Trout Creek warned of, but indeed, the traffic was light with very few trucks. Had it not been, that portion would have been torment.

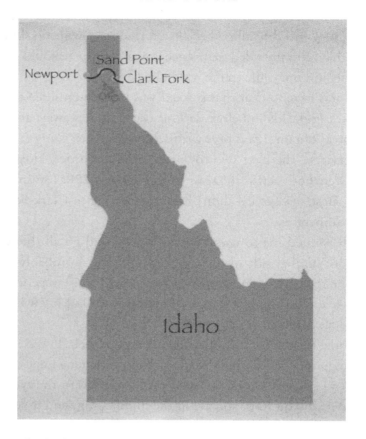

Eight miles before Clark Fork, I crossed the border into Idaho. I had to ride several hundred yards to get to the "Welcome to Idaho" sign. It was difficult terrain, even for the highway department to provide a turn-out for the welcome sign.

It took three of my meal bars to get to Clark Fork, and I was starving. I stopped at the first place I came to: the My Place Café. I was super bummed that it had closed about 10 minutes earlier. I went ahead to the Cabinet Mountain Bar. I almost backed out the door when it looked more like a bar than a food place, but I stayed and had an excellent Mushroom Swiss burger. Afterward, I went to a store and bought a beer for my first Idaho stealth camp.

It would be dark a little earlier because of extremely heavy overcast. About three miles out of town, I found a little loop road that dipped down below some bushes. It was somewhat trashy but good enough. It featured a terrific view of Lake Pend Oreille. I put the tent up replete with rainfly. Rain was imminent.

Tomorrow, I would be hooking up with US Highway 2. It would be a reunion for me as I had an unusual adventure along that highway back in my hitchhiking days.

77 miles.

Some time ago, I was crossing the continent from west to east after a summer of working at the cannery in Alaska. On that trip I intended to hitchhike from Seattle to Providence, Rhode Island and then down to Sarasota, Florida.

I visited Banff and Edmonton, then dropped down from Canada to Highway 2 near Havre, Montana. By the time I hitched to Williston, North Dakota, many people giving me rides had suggested, "You ought to hop a freight train." Hmmm, OK.

Williston had a large rail yard with lots of train traffic. I sat in the yard in the evening and watched the trains. It was a very cold, 18-degree night.

Back then every freight train had a caboose. I watched a westbound train roll in, but it only stopped for a few seconds and changed engineers. Then it rolled out of the station, and when the caboose reached the station, it slowed down enough for the conductors to swap by running alongside. It looked dicey, but I thought I would give it a go.

I walked a long way to the west of the station. My hope was that when the train stopped to switch engineers, I would be close enough to an open boxcar to hop in. It was new to me, and I had no idea how stupid this plan was.

First, there was no such thing as a printed freight train schedule. I had no idea when to expect an eastbound freight. The next two trains were both westbound! I thought I was going to have to spend a frigid night in this rail yard.

Finally, there came an eastbound freight. It slowed down but did not stop to change engineers. Though it had slowed, it was going too fast for my gimpy ass to get on a freight car. I jogged along as one empty boxcar after another passed me. Each time I had to let them go, but the train was slowing more.

The other caveat in this undertaking was that the bottom of an open door of a boxcar was about sternum height. I would have to sling my pack in and then, hopefully, climb in myself. How many ways could that go wrong?

Eventually, a boxcar rolled along with the door on my side latched open. I slung my pack in and then seal-hopped through the door.

I was somewhat comforted by the fact that me and my pack were in, but then the train slowed to a stop. Oh well. I was indoors of sorts, sweating, freezing, and exhausted. I would spend the night in this boxcar regardless.

I wrapped up in my sleeping bag to warm up. The train backed up, went forward, and backed up again. There was some switching going on, and I was resigned to being put on a side track for the night. After a while, the train started going again. Thankfully, headed east. I got up and sat in the open doorway for a while. We went through several crossings, and I waved if there were any cars. It was late. We were picking up speed all the while, and I had to give up the fun of sitting in the doorway as it turned insufferably cold.

I got back in my sleeping bag as we flew down the track. I can't say I was comfortable because we were rocketing down the rails at such speed that, from time to time, I was lifted off the floor of the boxcar. I don't know how long I slept or if I slept at all. After a number of hours, the train stopped, and a string of freight cars, including mine, was put off on a siding. It was still dark, so I slept in my boxcar until morning.

When I got up and looked out the door of the boxcar, I could see nothing but field where I thought Highway 2 should be. It was apparent that I was in a large rail yard. In a boxcar with only one door open, you can't see what is out the other way. I decided that I had to leave and see what happened. I presumed I might be arrested, but I was not going to stay in the boxcar until nightfall.

I had to cross several railroad tracks under freight cars—taking my backpack off and dragging it under. I could see why they might not want people hopping freights. It was inherently dangerous on or off. I finally made my way to a road that was heading south out of the rail yard. Many railroad workers saw me. Some waved; some gave me the stink-eye. I walked at least a mile until I came to a paved road running east/west. I presumed it was Highway 2, and I started hitchhiking east. The very first car that picked me up was a lone male driver who said, "You ought to hop a freight." I told him I just had, and I added that the funny thing is when you get off the train you don't know where you are. He smiled, but he did not understand what I was getting at.

So I asked, "Where am I?"

He laughed and said, "You're in Minot!"

Today, I was going to get on Highway 2 headed in the other direction. It would be a short riding day. Ed, my wife's brother's wife's brother, lives in Dover, Idaho, which was just a little past Sandpoint. It would be nice to stop there.

I had driven a car through Sandpoint about 20 years ago, and I thought it was as beautiful as could be. After that, when people would say, "Mmmmm, Coeur d'Alene, beautiful," I would always counter with, "No... Sandpoint."

This morning the sky was heavily overcast with light rain predicted. Luckily, it was dry when I got out of the tent to break camp. I put on my rain gear and departed from what would be my last campsite for a while. As I set out, it sprinkled drops, and I hoped it didn't get worse. But by Hope, Idaho, it turned into real rain. Five miles from camp, I found what looked like a convenience store in East Hope and hauled in there. It was the Holiday Shores Resort and Marina. I had a difficult time getting out of my rain outfit under a tiny awning in the pouring rain. When I went inside, I found that it had convenience store-like accoutrements, a grill that was not in use, and nice inside seating. I was ecstatic to find breakfast burritos and good coffee. I took my repast to one of the tables. There was a threesome at another table, the only other patrons. They were having some kind of meeting, and I was still there when the meeting ended. Two men stayed behind and engaged me in conversation. One of them was from California, and the other was a local. They were a little younger than me. We talked about everything from bicycle travel to fishing on Lake Pend Oreille.

I probably stayed there an hour, but I didn't quite wait out the rain. As I was leaving, I had to don my rain gear again though it wasn't raining as hard. It was still heavily overcast, and more rain seemed likely. The road was getting trafficky. After about 10 miles, the rain quit for good. Another nine miles after that, I was in the Ponderay/Sandpoint area.

When I was in Coeur d'Alene 20 years ago, it was, to me, hideous traffic congestion in a beautiful setting. It did not appeal to me. At that time Sandpoint was a beautiful backwater area.

Perhaps I had said too many times, "No… Sandpoint." It had caught on by now. It was a profusion of automobiles in a supreme setting. For me it had lost most of its charm though the downtown had a little left.

I had a great lunch and then biked over to a coffee shop to get an Americano and catch up on my communication. Ed, my next host, was at work and would not get home until evening. He lived in Dover, six miles away. I relaxed and posted to my GoFundMe and dropped texts to other people who were following me in spirit. I found out that my brother Bill and our friend Jim intended to meet me in Spokane the next evening. That put a little pressure on because it was more than 70 miles from Ed's house to Spokane. Barring any unusual circumstance, it would be doable.

There is a Sandpoint to Dover Community Trail that was very convenient for getting out of town. GMB suggested the route. It was terrific and avoided traffic, but it did not go all the way to Dover. A foot bridge that the app seemed to think was there was not there, and I had to "feel" my way around some neighborhoods to get back on Highway 2.

When I turned onto Ed's road, I found that he lived very high up on a very steep, dirt road. It was a road I could not ride up under the best of circumstances. I pushed the bike for over a half mile when a guy came along in a pickup truck and asked me if I was alright. I told him I was trying to get to Ed's house, but I was just too old.

He offered, and I accepted my first bicycle transport ride of the trip. I wanted to be able to say I pedaled every inch of the journey, and I justified this by noting that when I got back down to Highway 2, I would still be covering every inch—this was just a side-trip. Anyway, he knew Ed and dropped me off at the house where there was a "Welcome, Ken" sign in the driveway.

It was a beautiful house that Ed had built on the side of the mountain. Everything about it was artistic. The view out the back was stunning, and there were imaginative touches throughout.

I lounged around as recommended until Ed got home. When he arrived, we hit it off immediately. By profession he fights forest fires, so there was plenty of discussion about that. He is well-traveled and extremely well-read. He ran mountain trails for fun, and we had a terrific rapport.

His wife was away for the week, and I was sorry I did not get to meet her. She is an artist, and the house teemed with her creative works. I loved it there. Ed and I stayed up and talked until it was too late for both of us.

25 miles.

In the morning Ed made a great breakfast, and I did dishes and cleaned up after he left for work. I was thankful to have such an inspiring interlude, but now for a day of riding that would end up in my last state.

Newport, Washington was just 26 miles away. Highway 2 traveled along the Pend Oreille River the whole distance to Newport. It was beautiful riding under a partly sunny sky and a perfect temperature. The automobile traffic wasn't bad because this would not be the route that most people would choose for going between Sandpoint and Spokane. However, it was the best scenic route between the two, and I was glad to be on it.

CHAPTER 18

Odyssey Adds Argonauts

I didn't stop in Priest River. Newport is a much bigger place and would have more services. Besides, I wanted to get a lot of miles behind me to increase the odds of my making it to Spokane before dark. In-between Priest River and Newport, I encountered one more Caligula. Another diesel pickup truck stench-master. There was not a lot of wind, so I ended up riding in the deliberate smogging for 100 yards. Dang—that screwed up the averages. The Caligula count was now even with my first cross-country trip. I can't imagine the satisfaction that Cal got out of that. Maybe I could if I was a poorly brought up four-year-old.

I crossed the Pend Oreille River for the last time before I rode into Newport. Interestingly, though, I had not crossed that water course for the last time. From here the river travels north all the way into British Columbia. It curves back down, and just before reentering the United States, it joins the Columbia River. I would certainly be encountering the flow of water again later.

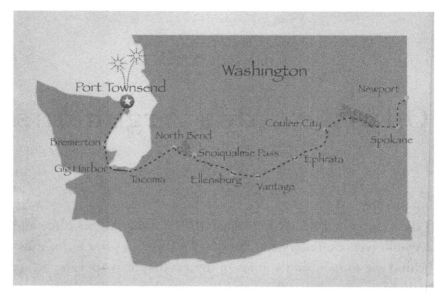

The city of Newport is divided by the state line. A little piece of the town sits in Idaho and the rest in Washington. I wondered how they handle that at the DMV. Anyway, I was more interested in capturing the "Welcome to Washington" sign in a photo with Truckee. I managed to miss it, and at the Safeway Supermarket, I stopped to ask about it. I assumed there had to be one, but everyone was very friendly, and no one was sure. Of course, it would be something that all these locals would be taking for granted. A lady pointed diagonally across a nearby busy intersection and guessed it would be over there.

Sure enough, I had cut through some parking lots to get to Safeway and missed it because it was an unconventional welcome sign for this trip. The sign was perched over the highway right where I might have expected if I wasn't looking for the more usual billboard-style sign.

I parked Truckee on the sidewalk and crouched down to include the sign with the bike. Now it was time for some food.

In keeping with my usual modus operandi, I looked in the app for a place on the far side of town that might still be serving breakfast. I found it in Audrey's Restaurant—a mom-and-pop type of place. It was perfect. The service was fine, the food was fine, plenty of coffee, and I got to sit indoors.

Now it was time to boogey. 47 miles to go to Spokane. Highway 2 rose and fell, but it was flattening out compared to most of the topography I had encountered over the last weeks. After Spokane, I would be in the Columbia Basin, and the terrain would be the opposite of what western Montana and the panhandle of Idaho were like. I would be headed toward the Cascade Range.

I toyed with the idea of following down the Columbia River and avoiding the mountains. But that would add a couple hundred miles to the trip. I had a while to think about it. It was going to take me three or four days to cross the Basin.

At one point I stopped at the top of a grade to grab a snack out of my bags and adjust my gear. A policeman pulled up behind me and stopped. I walked back to his car and told him I was all right. He asked some questions about my trip. "...Yes, Florida." He said he was inspired. All five of my encounters with law enforcement on this trip were benevolent and kindhearted.

As expected, traffic was picking up, and the road was widening. GMB had some suggestions for getting off Highway 2, but I wasn't buying it. 2 was the straightest route toward the downtown, and it was getting late. My brother Bill texted and said they would not get there until after dark. They asked if I could find a motel for the three of us.

I called the Baymont Inn and Suites. They were reasonably cheap, and the gal on the phone answered the two questions correctly: ground floor, non-smoking? "Yes." And was there free parking? "Yes."

When I arrived, the desk clerk told me she was mistaken—I had to take two rooms on an upper floor. "Oh, and the parking garage is closed for repairs." Effectively, there was no ground-floor room, and parking was on the street. One of the problems of bicycle travel is that at the end of a long day, you don't feel like riding all over looking for particular needs. You just want to get someplace and be there.

227

I took the room keys but found that the bicycle would not fit in the tiny elevator. Bill and Jim were bringing two bicycles. In downtown Spokane I don't think anyone would risk leaving a bike on a car outside.

I returned to the front desk and explained the problem. Suddenly, she was able to come up with two adjacent ground-floor rooms.

I don't fully understand motel shenanigans. I mean, I know they want to fill rooms, but to what degree of honesty? I remember that while I was in the lobby of the motel in Missoula, I overheard the desk clerk—the same one I had reserved with—telling a prospective client on the phone that he only had one room left. That was exactly what he told me when I made my reservation two hours before.

I walked across the street to Molly's Family Restaurant, which sounded perfect. I was starving. The doors were locked with no indication as to why. There wasn't even the usual "help wanted" signs. Again, I couldn't waste energy looking for particulars, so I walked kitty-corner across the street to Taco Bell. I did not have the gumption to travel farther than that.

When Bill and Jim arrived, we didn't do anything celebratory. They had driven all the way from the San Francisco Bay area, and I had biked far. We didn't have the oomph to commemorate the beginning of our enterprise. We settled in for the night at the Baymont Inn and Suites.

73 miles.

We left early, in part because we had to leave before the parking meters became active. Both guys had bikes, and the plan was that one of them would drive the car, and the other would bike with me. They were not used to the kinds of miles I was doing, so I carried all my gear. I felt like putting any of my gear in the car would be cheating. Jim cycled a lot back home, and he brought a very fast road bike. My brother Bill had a mountain bike with touring-style tires on it. He also had some hip issues, so Jim did more of the bike riding. I let them work all of that out. I just kept riding as they switched back and forth. They were determined not to interfere with my trip, but instead just to take part in it.

We all rode together for a way at first. It was a convivial start. After several miles, Jim rode back to get the car. Bill and I had a long slog out of town going up a seemingly endless grade. It was a tough first ride for Bill.

I had decided to ride across the Columbia Basin on Highway 2. Since they only wanted to cooperate, the plan was the same as was my usual—keep riding, see how far we got.

Once you get west of Spokane, the terrain is desert-like with huge intervals that are flat. The traffic goes from fast moving-congestion to merely bad. It is amazing how far you must get away from Spokane before the traffic din settles down to tolerable. I had my meal bars and usual stuff. I sort of didn't want to acknowledge that I had a possible "support" vehicle. They didn't carry any of my stuff, but it was a support vehicle in subtle ways. Whoever was driving could go ahead and suss out places to eat and places to stay. We stopped for lunch in Reardan at Dean's Drive-In. They weren't allowing inside seating yet, but we sat outside in very comfortable weather. The gal who served us chimed right in with our jubilant mood. We were all satisfied with what we got. It was a great stop.

We had an excellent day of riding and stopped for the night in Wilbur, Washington. I had not wanted to route myself through Grand Coulee at the Hoover Dam because I had been there long ago, but Bill and Jim wanted to see it. Bill found on the internet that the visitor's center at the dam was open until 9 p.m. We decided to side-trip up there in the car. Except for that short ride up the mountain at Ed's house, I had not ridden in a car since Denver, three weeks ago. Still, I had managed to cover a lot of ground in that time.

Of course, when we arrived at the visitor center, it was locked up tight. The internet still insisted it was open. Nevertheless, we enjoyed the spectacular site, and the round trip was fun.

We came back to Wilbur and had a nice meal at the Alibi Eatery and Pub near the motel. It was a terrific day. Having Bill and Jim along added a nice dimension to my odyssey. They did not impede my progress; they enhanced it.

64 miles.

We had breakfast at Doxie's Diner and then headed out into some tough headwinds. We were badly in need of a rest by the time we got to Hartline. It was difficult to get out of the wind and the sun, so we went into town and lay out behind a school.

Just outside of Coulee City, we stopped to talk to a young man walking with a backpack. He was walking (not hitchhiking) to Michigan and then to Florida. Wow! I couldn't imagine doing that. I have a difficult enough time staying hydrated with my much better range. I don't know how the walkers do it crossing these hot, dry landscapes. I gave him a bottle of water and a meal bar. I also gave him my contact information for when he got to Florida and wished him farewell.

In Coulee City we needed a break from exerting against the wind and stopped at the community park. I found a nice spot on a bench in the gazebo and had a nap. Afterward, we went to Couleegan's Bar and Grill for lunch.

This was an important route decision point. There are only so many places to cross the Columbia River. One option was to continue west on Highway 2 from here and cross at Wenatchee. From there we could continue on Highway 2 all the way to Seattle. The downside to that option would be that the road would be much narrower and hillier getting through the Cascade Range. Also, Stevens Pass, the highest point on that route, is a thousand feet higher than Snoqualmie Pass on I-90. I was trying to limit my elevation gains as much as possible.

From Coulee City we had a choice to cross the waterway and follow down 17 on the western, windy side or go out behind town on Pinto Ridge Road, eventually connecting to Highway 28 into Soap Lake. We chose Pinto Ridge Road because GMB said "mostly flat."

The stiff wind was bad enough, but the road turned out to be a combination of super-fast downhill spots with incredibly long, grinding, slow, wretched upward parts. It was anything but flat. It was brutal. We wondered how GMB could have it so wrong.

Riding into Soap Lake, Washington was a welcome relief. Bill found us a nice suite at the Masters Inn. We unpacked our bikes, got cleaned up, and headed to the Del-Red Pub. It was an excellent place. The young lady that waited our table came to see what we needed and then ran back to the kitchen. We were nobody to her, but she did not act like it. This was a small-town eatery, but the service was above and beyond.

57 miles.

The next morning, the plan was to get some miles behind us and have breakfast in Ephrata. Riding into Ephrata, Bill and I had somehow missed the Country Deli. When we connected with Jim, he mentioned it, and he abandoned the car to ride back with us. We all pulled up on our bicycles out in front of the place. A lovely young lady was walking out of the restaurant with some to-go food. I asked her if they were serving inside, and she said in a Hispanic lilt, "For you they are." She and her guy and all of us got into a great conversation on the lawn. Though they were in a car, they were bike riders, and we had a lot to talk about. During the course of the conversation, we talked about my experience with the possible tornado in western Kansas. The fella reiterated what I had heard from others—that one shouldn't hide in a viaduct during a tornado. At the time there had been no other options. Just a very shallow ditch and flat ground. I don't think I will ever understand the logic.

At any rate we went in past the "help wanted" signs and had a terrific albeit slow breakfast. The place was crowded, and the waitress did the best she could all by herself. I think the kitchen guy was also by himself.

After breakfast, we got onto Highway 28 to hook up with Highway 283 toward George, Washington. On the way out of town, a very little dog chased me with amazing small-dog determination. I could only just stay ahead of him. It was the first dog pursuit since before crossing the Mississippi River. He chased me with such obstinacy that I didn't have the heart to spray him with dog repellent.

The wind was similarly unfriendly. We were happy to take a break at the Sage Coffee House and Bistro. The ladies inside gave us the excellent advice to use the frontage road on the southern side of I-90 to stay off the Interstate for another six miles.

We stopped for a photo op at the sign for the town of George, Washington. Bill didn't really want to ride on the Interstate Highway, so they swapped out. Too bad for Bill. We were finally getting some relief from the battle with the wind because we would drop 600 feet in elevation over the next eight miles.

There were excellent views of the Columbia River on the way down, and there was even a nice rest area overlook for the westbound side of the highway. It was delightful to not have to pedal so hard, but, of course, payment would be exacted on the other side of the river. Ellensburg, Washington is 1,542 feet above sea level. There would be at least a 900-foot gain.

We had often discussed the third option of staying along the Columbia River all the way to Vancouver, Washington. It would average out to be downhill with no passes to climb. That appealed to me, but it would add 360 miles. That did not.

We stopped to survey the bridge over the Columbia River. The unfortunate part of riding the interstates is that when they make a bridge over water, the beautiful, wide, safe shoulder is relinquished. Sometimes it is reduced in width, and sometimes it is taken away altogether. In this case there was a very small shoulder, and it was strewn with debris all the way across. The traffic was extremely heavy and extremely fast. It would be impossible to cross safely on a bicycle.

Had Bill and Jim not been there with the car, I would have had to hitch a ride across or just follow down the river for the added 360 miles.

The bike rack was big enough for three bikes, so it was just a matter of getting us and all our junk inside. We packed up like sardines and drove across the Columbia River bridge.

The town of Vantage lies immediately on the west side of the Columbia River. We stopped at Blustery's Restaurant and chowed down. We had at least 900 feet to gain, but we did not realize that we were going to gain all of it and more right away. We left town on the Vantage Highway heading toward Ellensburg. The road started uphill right away and did not relent. There were no flat spots—it was all incline.

I was in my lowest gear the entire time. The good part was that I did not have to get off the bike and push. I could make the grade in low gear but had to stop and rest frequently. Bill was riding with me—Jim was driving.

Jim had gone ahead to reconnoiter. He came back and said the hill was eight more miles of up without any flat areas. Wow, eight miles—nothing but up.

Needless to say, I was not going to make it to Ellensburg or even Kittitas. There was nothing in-between us and these towns. Above us we could see a portion of a phenomenal array of wind turbines.

I gave up 16 miles from Ellensburg. Had I been alone, I would have set up my tent off of the road, but instead I loaded my bike on the car rack, and we drove to the Motel 6 in Ellensburg. The guys did not bring camping gear, and they didn't want to leave me alone out there.

We had an excellent dinner at the Sugar Thai restaurant.

57 miles.

We got up early and hit a Starbucks. Then we drove back to where we had stopped riding the night before. I was determined to be able to say I had ridden the entire distance across the country. But, oh yeah, I had just accepted a ride crossing the Columbia River.

Bill started out riding with me as they decided that he deserved some downhill after yesterday's grind up 8-Mile Hill. We were treated to a nice tailwind heading back to Ellensburg.

Near Kittitas we ran into a Thai couple that were riding loaded bikes in the other direction. They were heading for New York. It was Day 11 for them, Day 73 for me. They were just starting out on their long adventure, and I was nearing the end of mine. She was the one who, talking about the caloric expenditure on a trip like this, said, with the biggest smile, "Beer and ice cream for breakfast if you want."

The three of us rolled back into Ellensburg for breakfast, but we did not have beer and ice cream. We dined at the Palace Café, and we all agreed it was the best breakfast of our days together.

After that, we left Ellensburg for the second time. Once again, I got back on my old friend "Old Highway 10." This was a continuation of the road that had such magnificent views along the Yellowstone River back in Montana. Again, it is non-Interstate riding through beautiful scenery. This time we were riding up the Yakima River. It was a sunny Saturday, and there were places we could see people rafting on the river below. The moderate easterly wind still pushed us.

In Cle Elum we filled up on food at Mike's Tavern. There would be nothing for us between here and Snoqualmie Pass. The biking would be all Interstate Highway with no services.

GMB suggested the Iron Horse Trail, a trail that goes across the state on an old railroad grade. I was pretty sure it wasn't paved, and I didn't trust it. I had asked the Thai couple about it. They said it was pretty good on the other side of the pass, but I needed a more fulsome recommendation than that. Especially seeing that they were riding on much wider tires than mine.

I made one last stop at Safeway on the way out of town. I wanted to get a giant iced coffee to help propel me to the pass. It was 30 miles further with a gain of 817 feet with most of the gain toward the end. The traffic was very heavy—a surging torrent of trucks. In a few places where they had to squeeze the highway through some narrows, the shoulder lane was reduced to four feet. It is plenty of room, but somewhat distressing given the rushing stampede of truck traffic.

The road flattened and widened along the peaceful-looking Keechelus Lake. We were having good weather, but that was predicted to change tonight. I wanted to get to the top before it did.

Jim had ridden the whole way from Cle Elum. He is in terrific shape, but that is a slog. And he hadn't ridden every day for the last two months like I had. He was probably pretty tired when he took a spill at an off-ramp we were taking for a rest stop. I didn't see him fall because I was far behind him. When I got there, I saw a series of punctures in his calf. Clearly, his front sprocket had bitten him.

I don't carry a first-aid kit. It was one of the sacrifices I made avoiding weight. I always have alcohol swabs, though, so I was able to clean it up for him. He wasn't too worried about it, and we got back on the bikes to head for the summit.

As we got to the top, it was getting dark. Heavy clouds moved in. The guys and I would be parting here. They had to get back to California, having lives other than biking. They wanted to get some miles behind them in the car as they had a long drive ahead. I assumed I was going to stay in my tent. I didn't know there was a motel up there, but Jim bought me a room at the Summit Inn as a parting gift. What a guy!

Jim got a flat tire in the parking lot of the motel—right at their finish line. Excellent timing. We had covered an impressive 256 miles during the four days we rode together.

We said our goodbyes in the parking lot. It felt weird to watch them drive off after our terrific adventure together. It was so good to have them for that part of the odyssey.

It was the off-season on Snoqualmie Pass, so there were not a lot of services open—but there were enough. The Summit Inn had a restaurant where I had a good meal. Then I walked across the street to the Dru Bru Brewery to check out their selection of dark beers. What more do you need? I was especially thankful for the room because it started to rain as predicted, and it poured down all night.

78 miles.

It rained all the next day too. I woke up to a heavy grey day. The weather app showed no hope of let up. I did not want to descend from the summit in rain, so I reserved a second night in the motel.

The rain slowed a little bit, and I tried walking up the road, but then the sky opened again. It was a misty, encompassing rain that prompted me to ensconce myself with my notes and my correspondence. The weather app said it was going to continue to rain in the morning, but I would don my rain wear and leave early anyway.

0 miles.

I hope that I have established that letting go of desires and fears brings peace and happiness—joy. Our minds constantly throw up wants, needs, and fears that distract us from our inherent peace. When I see this happening in myself, I can fight with the mind or just drop these things. Never fight them—just let them fall. It is not supposed to be like swatting flies. It is supposed to be like seeing that the flies did not exist in reality in the first place. That is truly letting go.

With practice the mysterious essence that I allude to can become as plain as day. When I have let go of everything, and I mean everything to a degree outside of imagination (imagination is just more mind), the essence is what remains, and I am unable to resist using words like love and joy.

We are humans so the ego will continue to pull the blinds. It calls for a relaxed kind of vigilance. An excellent tool for keeping the blinds wedged up (until I can remove them altogether) is thankfulness. On the internet there is seemingly endless discussion about the benefits of gratitude. All of it can truly be helpful though I am not convinced that one can be taught gratitude.

You can pass along a tradition of saying grace before a meal, but that is tradition and not necessarily felt gratitude. There is looking at someone who has less than me and feeling grateful. But that too is a kind of leveraging that will not get me far for long.

I can have gratitude for all the kind, generous people I met on my bike trip; for the friends that helped me along the way; for getting to cycle the Wind River Canyon; for a beautiful campsite along the Yellowstone River; or for being lucky enough to have friends join me. Life is richer for everything that I acknowledge with thankfulness though all those things are still egoistic.

I can be truly thankful that I survived the canoe accident; made it over Thorong La alive; missed the tornado or survived the orangutan encounter. Not to acknowledge those experiences with gratitude would be presumptuous to the point of debilitating. Some people are not thankful for much, and those lives are necessarily less satisfying. Everyone knows this on some level.

But that satisfaction also takes place at the level of ego. The thinking mind is still in charge and is permitting a type of indulgence. Of course, that life is far better than the unappreciative one. Gratitude is a transformational tool. Far better wellness will come from the gracious life for all concerned. It is better than nothing... or is it?

We are humans, but, more importantly, we are conscious beings. With our consciousness we observe all experience. Our consciousness sits behind our senses and sees the inputs. It sits behind the egoistic mind and observes its judgements, its foibles. It does not seem to be a thing in and of itself, but everything is what consciousness witnesses. There is heightened aliveness in our conscious presence. It is the primordial subject, and everything else is objects—observed things.

Releasing my mind of its primacy in my life—letting consciousness have the lead—takes me to sublime peace and joy. Ultimately, I will find myself grateful and for "no" "thing" in particular—the sincerest, deepest gratitude. It can only happen in what Eckhart Tolle refers to as "the now," the "present moment."

I might ask, "But how will that help me in the future?" But there I go—I am back in the mind in an instant, imagining something that is nonexistent. I have been catapulted back into the figment of anxiety. I have given up on pure consciousness, which is what I am in my essence, and focused back on my mind, which is supposed to be a tool.

I still experience fear, as you will see, but it is in immediate situations—not the lay-awake-at-night mind-made stuff.

CHAPTER 19

Gut-Wrenching Descent

Indeed, I was out the door by six in the morning, and there was nothing open for coffee or breakfast. The forecast predicted intermittent rain all morning. I put on my rain gear and went down the ramp on I-90 and was immediately terrified. The road was wet, which amps up the danger for biking. And the road grade was steep and super-fast. It called for a lot of braking, but with wet brakes. The temperature was in the low 40s. I should have been cold, but I was warmed by primal fear. The traffic was extremely heavy with nearly constant trucks, and the shoulder was narrowed in spots.

I wondered if there would be black ice. Back when I lived in Kodiak, Alaska, this could be black ice conditions. Patches of ice could form on damp roads even above 32 degrees. It put cars in the ditches without any warning.

Then I noticed the vehicles going gangbusters probably weren't worried about it because there was so much traffic, they had dried the road. Only the shoulder was wet.

I remembered all the banana slugs I had seen in this part of the country. For a lot of this descent, I was going too fast to reliably steer around debris. Would I need to avoid one of these giant slugs, or could I run over it without being bounced into traffic? They get to be almost 10 inches long, and they are terrifically slimy. If I tried to brake on one, would I slide into oblivion?

I wondered if I would be the first person ever killed by a banana slug. Not fright... terror!

I was not in a hurry, but traveling at, literally, breakneck speed. It was electrifying. Where was my joy now? It was buried under consternation. This could end well, but it didn't feel like it would.

It was very steep at first, but then smoothed out some. Still, there was not much pedaling involved until I turned off at the first North Bend exit where I was relieved to be back to sane biking. I knew that the rest of this trip was going to be mostly a trafficky mess with a few good bike trails, or so I thought. But right now, I was looking for you-know-what... breakfast and coffee. A place to untangle my nerves. This had been the most terrifying part of the trip. Tornados in Kansas could not compare.

I looked for the breakfast restaurant where Fred had taken me the last time I was here, but I couldn't find it. North Bend is not that big, but I did not know it well. This would have been a very high point of the trip for me because I had been here several times before visiting Fred at his house. I had worked with him in Alaska and had even fished on his salmon seiner. We had a wonderful bond that was unhinged by his passing several months before I left on this trip. A heavy nostalgia carried me to town. Instead of staying here for two or three days of excellent companionship, I was now relegated to just passing through.

I stopped at Huxdotter Coffee and had breakfast and an Americano. I took a lot of time because I was recovering from that helter-skelter descent.

I spent some time comparing the two major passes. From Cle Elum to Snoqualmie Pass, I only had to gain 860 feet over 30 miles. It was a breeze compared to Homestake Pass at the continental divide back in Montana. There I had to gain 1,800 feet in only 13 miles. There is really no comparison. The descents were also incomparable.

Back in Montana, descending from the pass, I dropped about 800 feet in 10 miles. Today's fall was 2,760 feet in 25 miles. 80 feet per mile compared to 92 feet per mile at Homestake. Perhaps that doesn't sound like that big of a difference, but the Montana decent was dry as a bone, which meant dry brakes. Today, there wasn't a dry bit of road shoulder all the way down. I was glad I didn't have to test any banana slug theories.

I left North Bend wanting to get through the Seattle/Tacoma area and get on the other side of the Tacoma Narrows. I wished to get the city/suburbs behind me and to start up the other side of Puget Sound toward Port Townsend. This desire led to me making my final big routing mistake.

If one was in a car and wanted to take the shortest route, they would get on I-90 West and get off in two exists to go south on Highway 18. Fortunately, I could stay on North Bend Way for several more miles to avoid some Interstate travel. I got back on I-90 for one short bit before getting off at Highway 18. This is where I made an egregious navigational error similar to the one I had made back in Colorado on Highway 86.

GMB did not offer Highway 18 as an option. Just as it had not offered Highway 86 west as a route back in Colorado. Both were clearly the shortest routes on the paper maps. They were both siren calls for unsuspecting cyclists. I guess GMB was trying to warn me, but it had misled me so many times by now that I didn't listen.

I rode down Highway 18 for a while trying to see what the problem might be. It was extremely trafficky, but with beautiful riding on a nice, wide shoulder… more siren song.

The weather couldn't seem to decide if it wanted me wet or not. There were occasional light sprinkles. After several miles, the shoulder shrank to barely tolerable. Tolerable to a XC cyclist can be pretty small.

However, that this route decision was likely a mistake was becoming evident.

Then it became obvious.

The shoulder all but disappeared in extremely heavy, fast traffic. I pulled off into a tiny parking area for a trail head. There were a couple of cars parked there and a locked bar gate across some kind of access road to the ridge on my west side. I tried to figure out between my map apps where the access went. It had all the signs of being a tour-biking mistake. There was no one around to ask.

I walked back to survey the highway to figure out what to do. I walked a little in the direction I was heading and could see up ahead that the road shoulder disappeared altogether. Altogether! In this massive traffic it would be certain injury or death. Continuing would be idiotic. Traffic in both directions was extremely heavy, so crossing and going back was not going to be an option either. Ughhh! The megalopolis!

I have never been fond of riding the shoulder against traffic. With a wide shoulder I might do it for a few hundred feet and still feel uncomfortable. There was very little road shoulder going backward now and none going forward. I rested in the small safe harbor for a while, hoping one of these vehicle owners would show up and tell me where this dirt road went. One of the cars had a bike rack on it, so I guessed that they went up the road on a bike, but most likely a mountain bike. The way around the gate was only barely passable on foot or by dragging an empty bike. It was going to be a lot more trouble for me. And if I did get on the other side of it, where in the hell would it take me?

One of the map apps seemed to think that this access led up to a trail that would follow along the highway—but up on the mountainside above it. From that trail it looked like I could later access the highway again. Hopefully where better conditions prevailed. First, I would have to strip my gear from the bicycle and portage around the gate. It was the best of a selection of woeful options.

I pulled up to the gate to start the disassembly, and a fellow with a mountain bike and three dogs showed up on the hill above. One of these parked cars was his. Probably the one with the bike rack. At any rate he could give me some answers.

Matt was a biking lover and a dog lover, so we were instant kin. He was able to size up the predicament I was in with little explanation. He knew that the biking situation on Highway 18 was atrocious for miles. However, I should add here that even regular cyclists shy away from roads that the XC cyclists find tolerable.

He said his bike rack could easily accommodate another bicycle, and even with the three dog kennels, we would be able to get all my crap in the car. He offered to drive me down a few exits to get to where the highway was reasonable for biking again. This meant that I would have taken up another offer of a ride on my XC trip. The first being the ride across the Columbia River. It meant another complication in the story of my ride all the way across the country.

I accepted gratefully.

Matt was heroic in his patience and willingness to get all my junk in his car around the three dog carriers. The dogs were patient too. On the way down the highway, he told me about living in Europe for a while and how he received a lot of help. He was happy to pass along some of that beneficence.

I think he would have taken me all the way to Tacoma, but I asked him to drop me off at the second exit. I could see that the road shoulder had returned to an adequate width. Thank you, Matt!

Now I was back to the love side of my love/hate relationship with Google Maps Bicycle. I knew that it would reliably guide me through the megalopolis on decent roads and any available bike paths. I just wished that it would steer me around unnecessary hills where possible. The app does not have a filter selection for youthfulness.

I got off Highway 18 in Auburn, Washington. I was quite happy to close that chapter of poor routing decisions. There were only the occasional drops of rain now, but the heavy overcast and threatening look of the sky continued.

I stopped at the IHOP on Outlet Collection Way for my second breakfast. After that, I stopped at the Starbucks next door for my second Americano. Starbucks got its start in Seattle at the Pike Place Market. By the time I first heard of it, Howard Schultz had purchased the company from the founders. Long ago, I passed through the Seattle area on the way to my work in Alaska, and Starbucks was big news. In his book about its origins, Schultz said he was inspired by his café experiences in Italy and considered changing the name to Il Giornale, which meant The Daily in Italian. I wonder how different the corporation would have turned out if he had ignored the advice of his close associates and changed the name.

Starbucks was close to the "Interurban Trail." Thank goodness for the forward-looking people who think up and implement these public paths. They kept me off the roads for about four miles of city, and then with GMB I found my way over to the Pacific Highway East. It was a thoroughfare but a pleasant ride for about four more miles until I had to start making my way toward the Tacoma Narrows Bridge.

There isn't a good "magic bullet" route to the bridge. I found myself winding around and going up and down some steep "walk-the-bike" hills. Really, it was unpleasant traveling. Getting out of the city became more and more attractive.

I was happy to finally arrive at the Tacoma Narrows Bridge. Though it would not mean the end of urban sprawl, in terms of traffic, it might mean diminishment.

The original Tacoma Narrows Bridge, "Gallopin' Gertie," was built in 1940, but blew down only four months after it was opened. Its collapse influenced the science and engineering of all long-span bridges thereafter. The original has been replaced by two huge bridges that provide for an enormous amount of traffic on the Kitsap Peninsula. The bridges include a bodacious, protected crossing for pedestrians and bicycles. At the far western end of the bridge, there is a climb in elevation that I couldn't ride. I guess I was too optimistic in thinking that, once I got over the Cascades, I wouldn't be walking my bike anymore.

Toward the top, a man named Tom grabbed the bike to help me finish the ascent. I could have made it on my own, but it was awesome that he jumped in and helped me. I was glad that spontaneous kindness had not ended. Thank you, Tom!

It was late enough in the day that I set my sights on the cheapest motel near Gig Harbor. I figured if I could find a stealth camp before then, it would be great, but I was in a populated area now, and stealth camping would be challenging. In confusion I did not set GMB for the actual motel but instead had it set for Gig Harbor. So, I missed my target motel, which was just off the route, and I ended up descending into town.

There was a lot of downhill to the water. Too much for me to go back up at this hour. I knew I was in fiscal trouble. The setting of Gig Harbor is idyllic. Everything about it screamed charm. There were plenty of things that indicated tourism—nice store fronts, marina, massage. Gig Harbor was around the corner from the madding crowd, but not that far. Stealth options were gone, and cheap places to stay were not to be found. Short of grinding my way back up to the main road, I was going to have to get a budget-breaking place.

I started to think back. Was I getting spoiled? I had not spent a night in my tent since back in… Idaho! Thanks to Ed, Bill and Jim, I'd been luxuriating since that little place on the side of the road outside of Clark Fork. I missed sleeping in my tent, but I wouldn't be setting it up tonight in Gig Harbor. I was too deep into civilization and too tired to rescue myself.

I pulled into a motel across from the marina. The young lady at the check-in said, yes, they had a room available. She didn't seem to think anything of me not having a vehicle license plate number to put on the registry. When I showed her my Florida driver's license and said I had ridden my bike from there, she just smiled. Hmm, perhaps lots of people ride their bikes from Florida to Gig Harbor. She exuded niceness and goodwill, so I was happy to be there.

This was a splurge accommodation, but I did not require a splurge meal. In fact, my craving for steak seemed to have been satisfied permanently back in Montana. Now I just wanted something to eat that was close. El Pueblito was a cane-walk away, and I had a terrific meal there and excellent service. I would like to have walked around Gig Harbor a little more, but I was done. I needed to get back to my nice room and get my hand-laundry done.

73 miles.

I woke up knowing that I had only one more night on the road. Port Townsend was about 70 miles away, and barring any unforeseen cataclysm, I would be there the next day. I would have had to push to make it there today, but I did not want to push. I really wanted to take my time and spend the last night of my odyssey in my tent. I would shoot for getting across the Hood Canal Bridge and camping somewhere on the other side.

I packed up my bike and pushed it up to the motel entrance to partake of their coffee and other morning accoutrements. I retrieved a coffee and a yogurt and went up to talk to the woman behind the desk. After a minute, she said, "Oh, you're my bicycle guy!" She was the owner, and she said it was her daughter who checked me in last night. She said her daughter was very impressed and talked a lot to her about me. I told her that wasn't the read I got on the evening's check-in, but that her daughter was very nice and professional.

She and I talked a lot about my bicycle trip and how I ended up in Gig Harbor. During my second coffee, she loaded me up with health bar snacks and even gave me a discount on my room! I would have already recommended The Maritime Inn to anyone, but wow! Lovely, lovely people.

GMB put me on some great back roads to Port Orchard. It was a very nice area also, but it did not have quite the charm of Gig Harbor. There, GMB recommended that I get on the "foot ferry" to Bremerton at Annapolis. That sounded good. Who doesn't appreciate a boat ride?

When I got to the Annapolis dock, it was clear that nothing was going to happen there. It looked closed. I called up the ferry service, and they told me that the boat was not going to go from there—that I had to go to Port Orchard.

It was only a short ride, and I waited at the dock for the foot ferry to show up. There was a nice ramp, and I was happy that I was going to get my whole bike on there without having to break it down. However, when the ferry arrived, the crew told me that the elevator was broken on the Bremerton side and that they would not be allowed to help me get my bike up the stairs.

Okay. It was a plenty nice-enough day, and the ride around the end of the bay was not that long. Also, it was flat. I would say, though, that the path, though paved, was not well used or maintained. The thick blackberry bramble tore at my panniers.

After winding through Bremerton, I had a long, pleasant ride before getting on Highway 3. The roads were very busy to the Hood Canal Bridge with good shoulders. It is a nice floating bridge that more than accommodated bicycle traffic.

It was time to start looking for my last stealth camp. On the far side of the bridge, there was a turnoff to Port Ludlow and Termination Point Road. Termination Point Road had my name all over it for stealth camping, but there was an extremely steep hill leading down to the water. I was fairly certain that I did not want to face that hill first thing in the morning, so I pushed on.

The terrain was not conducive to stealth camping. The roadsides took turns being too steep up or too steep down for me to walk my bike into the woods. I turned on South Point Road and found a fire protection district building. It was a decent flat area, and there were two cars in the parking lot. I went up and knocked on the door to ask permission to camp there. There was no answer, which I took as permission.

I went behind the building and put up my tent replete with rain fly. The weather was extremely dank just as it had been every other time I had been on the Olympic Peninsula.

From my tent that night, I sent everyone following me this message: "I am going to end this trip at two p.m. at the Pope Marine Park in Port Townsend, Washington tomorrow (Wed 6/16/21). That will be Day 77, and I will have ridden 3,735 miles. Will somebody please call Ellen DeGeneres?!"

36 miles.

On my last day of riding, I broke camp with plenty of time to kill. I was only about 21 miles from Port Townsend and had most of the day to get there. This was the opportunity for another dumb decision... go to Port Ludlow for breakfast.

I backtracked to Teal Lake Road and subjected myself to some arduous climbs. It was beautiful, but I was ready to have all the "up" come to an end. As I dropped down from the top of some ridge into Port Ludlow, it was evident that I had made yet another mistake. The roads in Port Ludlow went either up or down. I don't think I encountered any flat spots.

Also, Ludlow was clearly a village for well-moneyed people. I made my way back to my breakfast restaurant target, but all the while seeing that I was going to end up out of my budget range. I was hungry, but a convenience store would do me. I decided to skip breakfast, eat a meal bar, and find my way back out to Highway 19.

After a while, I came upon a woman on the side of the road who shouted, "Ken!" I stopped, and a car passing by us occluded the sound of her first name, and all I heard was her last name, which triggered no memory. She had a beautiful, bright countenance. She said, "I am on my way to the city, and I thought I might see you."

I did not have the guts to admit that I had no idea who she was. She said that she worked at the health food store/farm stand in Chimacum and that she was going to call them and tell them to give me whatever I wanted for lunch on her. During the remaining conversation, I gathered that I had worked with her at the cannery in Alaska long ago. But I had worked there for decades, and I couldn't place which decade she belonged to. She was obviously connected to someone who knew I was on this trip.

She needed to get somewhere, so our encounter was brief. She said that she wanted to get a picture of us for Dara.

Dara is my triathlete trainer friend who advised me so well on my first cross-country adventure, Route 67. Now I knew what time frame to connect her to, but I met Dara at the cannery about 30 years ago. That was too far back for my powers of memory.

When I got to the store in Chimacum, I picked up a sandwich and a coffee, and the woman at the counter said, "Oh, you're Hillary's friend." Now I had another clue, but I couldn't access those memory cells either. Dara/Hillary... hmmm.

The folks at the store were very helpful, telling me about the bike route path to Port Townsend. GMB didn't seem to know about it. I found the trailhead and then immediately proceeded to get lost. I came out on South Discovery Road and got lost, found, and then re-lost.

Finally, I ended up on the Pacific Northwest Trail/Larry Scott Trail. I am thankful for guys like Larry Scott, but I could not find out that much about him. I was happy that his trail got me into the south end of Port Townsend in a traffic-free, scenic manner.

I still had time to kill until my designated arrival time at Pope Marine Park. Of course, this meant coffee. I knew where there was a café that I had been to many times before in previous visits. I even knew how to get there from the trail. Unfortunately, I remembered a place with inside seating, and now there was only an ordering window near some picnic tables. COVID!

I parked my bike and started to walk toward the window for ordering. The woman at the window—in a way that exactly split the difference between congeniality and command—asked me to put my mask on. Oh shit! I was on the West Coast now. For the first time since leaving Florida, I was met with this enhanced wariness of the coronavirus. It caught me off-guard. I said, "If I put a mask on, will you serve me coffee in a ceramic cup?" She did not feel the need to answer.

This part of the country had been devastated by the earliest wave of the pandemic. While the science was still being worked out, it made perfect sense to employ whatever methods—useful or not—that were thought to stem the spread. By this time, however, it was well known that catching COVID off surfaces was extremely unlikely.

I couldn't be served coffee in a ceramic cup, I was told, because they could not accept anything back through the window… except money. I had rarely run into this mentality since leaving Gainesville, Florida. Port Townsend is a tourist destination and steeped in it.

I found there was no sense arguing even though the logic of their stance seemed skewed to me. I had only to drink my paper-cup coffee. I was very happy to be there. It had turned into a wonderful, sunny day, and Port Townsend was beautiful.

CHAPTER 20

Finale

I arrived at the park exactly at two p.m. Ellen DeGeneres was not there, nor was Oprah. However, two friends were there on their bikes and two others as pedestrians.

Frank had shown up on his bike. He is the guy I was referring to when I told people I was just riding my bike over to my friend's house. I had met him at the cannery decades before, and we always remained in touch. We had biked together long ago in the Port Townsend area and again in Moab. And I had gone with him twice to deliver his tendering boat to Kodiak. The other guy on a bike had gone with us on one of those trips. There is no bonding (or unfastening for that matter) like a weeks-long boat trip. Charles and Frank and I had a terrific time on that cruise.

The other two of my greeting entourage I had never met. But a long, long-time mutual friend asked them to show up there on her behalf. I was extremely happy to meet them after hearing about them for years.

Someone suggested the brewery, and off we went. Frank is one of these fellows who knows everyone around, especially if they are involved in wooden boats. The legion of people I met at the brewery that afternoon were boaters, bikers, hikers, and rowers. They were a very active, adventurous crowd. One of them thought I stood out among the rest having ridden my bike from Florida. He called the local newspaper and told them that they "had to" interview me.

The weather stayed perfect for my five days in Port Townsend. It was nice to meet a lot of new people and to get reacquainted with Hillary. Alli Patton, a reporter for the *Port Townsend Leader*, bothered to track me down through Frank. She was a lovely woman from Alabama who seemed to get more inspired the longer we talked. She said it was unbelievable that a 69-year-old polio survivor had just ridden his bicycle 3,747 miles. I agreed with her. I sort of didn't believe it myself. Ironically, I did not feel like I had accomplished anything outrageous. I left my house in Florida and rode my bike most days for two-and-a-half months, ending up in Port Townsend, Washington. I wish I could revel in some kind of glory from that, but what I really know is that I am lucky. In biking parlance, it would be called an "unsupported" trip. In reality, my GoFundMe people helped me immeasurably both in finances and inspiration. And I rode my bicycle across the country on a route that was stippled with benevolent and generous people.

And the essence…

36 miles.

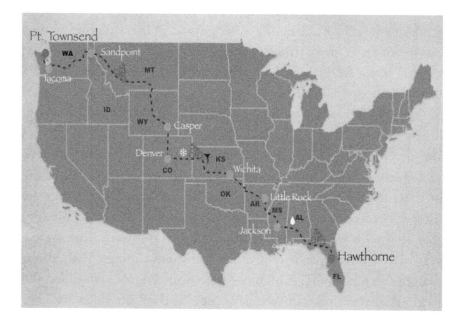

Epilogue

On Route 69 Truckee and I covered 3,747 miles over a total of 77 days. During that time, I took 12 days off riding either visiting folks or waiting out weather. I averaged about 57 miles per riding day. The most days I rode in a row were 26.

Days spent in each state: FL 6; AL 4; MS 8; AR 6; OK 6; KS 9; CO 9; WY 6; MT 13; ID 2; WA 9. The halfway point of the trip in distance was about five miles south of Hugo, Colorado. At the halfway point in time, I was holed up at the Sheridan Lake Federated Church in Sheridan Lake, Colorado.

I lost 27 pounds.

Made in the USA
Monee, IL
14 May 2024

58456075R00148